THE BURNING BUSH

THE BURNING BUSH

Signs of our Time

by

STUART Y. BLANCH

Archbishop of York

LUTTERWORTH PRESS

GUILDFORD AND LONDON

First published 1978

Those quotations taken from the New English Bible (2nd edition, 1970) are used by permission of Oxford and Cambridge University Presses

ISBN 0 7188 2346 X

Printed in Great Britain by
Richard Clay (The Chaucer Press) Ltd, Bungay, Suffolk

CONTENTS

To my wife, Brenda, and our family
and to the wider family of the
Northern Province.

INTRODUCTION

The reader is entitled to an explanation of the origins of this book and the particular form which it takes. No man can live and work on Merseyside without becoming aware of certain features of that physical and intellectual landscape. The tower block, the young vandal and the conurbation obtrude upon the consciousness; they are self-evidently signs of the times. But then no man can live in Yorkshire either, or in Pennsylvania, or Tanzania, or Peking, without becoming aware of certain other physical and intellectual features everywhere to be found in the twentieth century. Most of us at some time or other experience the departure lounge. We have all heard of Big Brother and we may even have taken part in a demo. These too are signs of our time, not confined to one particular nation or one particular culture. The initial reaction to most of the phenomena which are described in this book is one of disfavour. We wish they would go away − or that the 'experts' with which society abounds could somehow solve them. What are sociologists for, if not to heal the sicknesses of society? What are town planners for, if not to provide us with an agreeable environment? What are policemen for, if not to banish the vandal from the streets? But the signs abound, the problems expand rather than contract and we perish on a diet of disappointed hopes. It occurred to me, therefore, that there might be deeper causes for the phenomena which I describe here, that the minor eruption may suggest the huge seismic disturbance underneath, that we are in the presence of signs, not simply events.

The temptation to any Christian writer, and especially an archbishop, is to ask the questions to which he knows he has the answers – even if they are upside down at the back of the book. I have tried, with varying degrees of success, to resist this temptation. I have tried to look at the signs without any theological predilection, although of course it is theology which impels me to look at them as signs in the first instance. In each chapter (as I fear may be painfully evident to the reader) I have set out not knowing where I was going, trying to read the sign and then hear the message. This accounts for a certain diffusion of thought, for some repetition and inconclusiveness. The fact of the matter, as I have discovered, is that there are no 'solutions' to the problems we observe – and if there were it would be passing strange that the solutions which had eluded all the great figures of mankind should be suddenly vouchsafed to the observers and thinkers of the twentieth century. To have provided a solution therefore, at the end of each chapter, would have been to defeat the object altogether, which is to suggest range and depth in the superficial experiences which so alarm and disturb us. The tower block dominates the foreground, but behind it are the eternal hills. The young vandal screams his way through the streets, but he is simply an echo of the anguished voices of men and women down the ages. The departure lounge is the product of twentieth-century technology and of rapid intercontinental travel, but those who sit there have been sitting there since the beginning of time. I hope, therefore, that the reader will be patient with the mysteries which are as much beyond the comprehension of the wise as they are of the simple. Patience with mysteries, I have always believed, is the mark of the mature mind.

I acknowledge my debt to my secretary who typed and re-typed the script, to my lay chaplain who corrected the proofs, and to the countless others who in daily concourse, in prose and poetry, in theology and art, have helped me to read – however inadequately – some of the signs of our time.

THE FREEDOM FIGHTER

The freedom fighter, otherwise called the guerilla or terrorist (depending on whose side you happen to be) is a familiar figure in our world. He hijacks aeroplanes, he seizes hostages, robs banks, or assassinates rulers. He is seen on our television screens – elated and voluble when victorious, small and nondescript when defeated and in custody. To the honest citizen of the established democracies he is totally inexplicable, pursuing ends which seem hardly worth pursuing – and pursuing them with a kind of devious logic quite beyond the grasp of the quiet householder with his trim garden and his regular routines, a devoted family and friends at the golf club. An abyss of incomprehension lies between the terrorist who appears on the screen and the suburban house-holder in his easy chair.

But this, you may say, is just a passing phenomenon of the contemporary world, a dangerous fire fuelled by latent inequality which will in due course go out, leaving us to enjoy our pleasures as before. This is a comforting thought, but one which scarcely does justice to two facts. The first is that the civilization we now enjoy (or despise, as the case may be) is the product of a whole series of violent freedom movements. Cromwell, Robespierre, Garibaldi are the freedom fighters of a previous age, upon whose achievements such liberties as we enjoy are built. The second fact is that for every freedom fighter who captures a headline, or fills the screen in a brief moment of glory, there are a thousand who share his rage against society – sullen students on a university campus, bitter workers on the picket line, the angry playwright and the radical artist. These are all in pursuit of freedom, so called, who feel themselves trapped in a system which they did not create and have done nothing to deserve. Their political or industrial activity is more often the expression of this inner rage against society than of any rational plans to change it, or of any consistent political philosophy. The freedom fighter is a tiger at bay in his well-warmed, sumptuously provided cage waiting to spring upon the next unsuspecting keeper. Terrorism is the price we pay for the vivid discontents of so many of our contemporaries. A larger piece of meat or a degree or two on the central heating will not appease this tiger. He wants to be free. He wants to be back in his jungle. He wants to be his own master again, suffering hardship no doubt, but hardship by his own will, not comfort by the will of others.

Cromwell, Robespierre, Garibaldi ... the list might have been extended way back into history. The freedom fighter is no new phenomenon; he is a racial memory. So perhaps it is not as surprising as we might think that radical theologians sometimes claim Moses as the prototype of the freedom fighter. After all, did he not observe the burdens of his people and slay an Egyptian? The parallels are too obvious to be missed. Like so many freedom fighters in our own age, he was a member of an oppressed race but by a strange accident was himself spared the experience of oppression and was brought up in the oppressor's household. There is a sense in which he was the typical *emigré* enjoying the privileges of an establishment but all the time burdened with a sense of grievance on behalf of those to whom he belonged by

5

birth. The murder of the Egyptian was a gesture – no more – but a significant one in so far as it revealed the tension in the mind of a man who enjoyed his privileges and at the same time resented them. He had no plan for the liberation of his people. He was not even concerned with their liberation. The murder of the Egyptian was a cry of rage. Like most cries of rage it was unproductive and the only overt consequence of his action was a long exile. It was not the exile of a Trotsky in Mexico, busily writing memoranda, mobilizing his friends, criticizing the Pharaoh in Moscow; he was just a shepherd accustomed to his work, at ease and (in a measure) at peace with himself. He had done his thing. He had made his gesture. He would now grow his roses and mow his grass and travel up on the 8.30 for the rest of his days.

He was travelling up on the 8.30, as it were, going about his usual tasks, when he saw a bush that burned with fire but was not consumed. Long and tortuous have been the explanations of this remarkable event. But I think we would have to say that it lies too far back and too way out to be within our comprehension. All that one can say with certainty is that in that phenomenon, so banal and yet so striking, the God of the Universe spoke to him and called him to be a freedom fighter. We observe now how different the reaction is from that self-motivated, self-originating action with which Moses burst upon the scene of ancient history. No bold gestures now, but an only too obvious reluctance to take any action whatsoever. Every possible excuse is offered – he is not up to the task; the Pharaoh will not take any notice of him; his own race will not believe in him; he is a poor speaker and (he might have added) he has responsibilities to his family and to his present employer.

6

So it is a reluctant warrior who takes up arms on behalf of an oppressed people and ultimately delivers them from their oppressors.

I doubt if the radical theologians can justly claim Moses as their prototype. The author of the book of Exodus is a theologian of great distinction and a subtle observer of the human psyche. He wishes us to understand that there is a sharp distinction to be drawn between the self-appointed liberator in Egypt and the man who encounters in the desert a bush that burned with fire and was not consumed. It is as if Moses had to learn the inescapable lesson that freedom is not to be found through violence, or even successful gestures, but through the long maturing will of God, if it is to be true freedom. He had to learn another lesson too. He had to learn that a people freed from political oppression does not necessarily become free. For forty years the Hebrews remained trapped in the wilderness – trapped in futile longings for past material comforts, in their reluctance to believe in the promised land. They fought among themselves and manœuvred for personal power. Moses did not enter the promised land; he merely saw it from afar. He did not taste the milk and honey; to the end of his days he lived on wilderness fare, on insubstantial bread.

The author of the book of Exodus was handling the ancient traditions of his people in the light of experiences which were subsequent to the wilderness. He had the benefit of hindsight and he perceived that the theological principle which had been sketched out in the life of Moses had by his time been painfully etched into the life of the people of God as a whole. It was not by might nor by strength but by the spirit of the living God who had spoken to Moses in the bush, that freedom was to

7

be achieved. It was God who had convinced Pharaoh that he would have to let the people go. It was God who rolled back the sea and let the people pass. It was God who fed them with manna. It was God who caused them to walk dry shod across the Jordan, who scattered their enemies and settled them in. It is for this reason that the author dwells upon the patent inadequacies of Moses and spells out his reluctance to be responsible for his nation. He is not, distinctly not, the Mao tse-Tung of the ancient world, originating, planning, driving a great freedom movement. The 'long march' of Israel was not a triumph of the human spirit over the adverse forces of the world and of nature. It was a painful, long, drawn out, unenthusiastic trek of a small middle-eastern clan lurching from one crisis to the next and often bitterly regretting their freedom. But of such unheroic stuff, so the author would have us believe, freedom is made. The promised land is real; it lies there over the hills and across the river and in the highlands of Judea. The human author of their freedom sees it only from afar, but he does see it.

The Hebrews, on the whole, were not at home with abstractions. Unlike that other great formative influence of the ancient world, the Greeks, they did not engage in discussion about the nature of freedom, nor did they exalt it to the position it was at least formally afforded by Plato. The word most commonly used for freedom and its cognates in the Old Testament is a word otherwise associated with the manumission of slaves. To put it crudely, freedom meant liberation from actual slavery. You could buy it for money as the Tribune said he did, or you could be born free as Paul said he was.

So when our Lord came to the synagogue proclaiming the nature of his mission this was his theme – release to the captives, liberty for the oppressed. For the majority of his hearers that could have had only one meaning, given the political situation of the day. Here was another Moses about to liberate his people from the imperial yoke and to set the slaves free from the Pharaoh in Rome. There is in fact evidence from many passages in the gospels that our Lord was under pressure to do just this.

Up to the last moment his disciples were fondly hoping for it. Some of them may indeed have joined him with that end in view. No man could live in the Palestine of the first century without striking an attitude either reviling the Roman or coming to terms with him. The zealot and the tax collector in our Lord's company must have been uneasy associates.

It is against this background of political activism that we have to understand our Lord's discourse on freedom and to attempt to penetrate those enigmatic words, 'If the Son shall make you free, you will be free indeed.' It is evident that our Lord set his face consistently against confrontation with the Roman power, that he did nothing to encourage the familiar Messianic hopes of his followers, that he was unwilling to raise a banner for nationalism (if that was what freedom meant). In fact, he turned the concept of freedom on its head and spoke instead of a new slavery, of utter uncompromising obedience to himself and to him whom he represented on earth – the divine king in heaven. His followers were to be willing slaves of God most high, and therein to find the only freedom available on earth. Monarchy and servitude on earth are both a tragic parody of a perfectly legitimate relationship, even an essential one, for the human constitution. The man who rises in the market place or in the council chamber and shouts *Freedom!* knows full well that he is appealing to the deepest instinct of the human heart and can command a following. And so the government is overthrown and the regime is changed, the mighty are brought low and the lowly are raised – and poor suffering human beings merely exchange one kind of servitude for another. But the original call for freedom is right and the response to it is right. It has, however, to be qualified by the knowledge that the only freedom worth having is not to be achieved by political action but as the gift of God alone. It was God who set his people free by the hand of Moses. It was God who made Jesus of Nazareth free amidst a kingdom of slaves. It was God who set Saul of Tarsus free from the constraints of his own religious upbringing. 'Where the Spirit of the Lord is, there is liberty.'

The church thus finds itself in an ambivalent relationship with the freedom fighter. It applauds his motives, where they are free from mere power seeking. It admires his heroism and his willingness to sacrifice himself for the cause. It can never countenance slavery, whether it be of a political, commercial or industrial kind. But at the same time, it can never allow that this or that oasis in the desert is in any sense equivalent to the promised land. The Israelites would have been content enough to have stayed in an oasis in the desert. After all, there were giants in Canaan, there was the fearsome unknown across the Jordan, there were the great fortifications and walled cities. Could they not be content with freedom in the desert? It is for these reasons that I doubt whether any Christian can wholly commit himself to any so-called freedom movement which falls short of the freedom with which Christ has made us free. Our masters are not the men in pin-striped suits in Whitehall nor the grey men of the Kremlin; they are the spiritual forces of wickedness in higher places than either of those – and only the Son can set us free.

But how does he set us free and what is the nature of that freedom? Or, to put it another way, what is the promised land to which he beckons us? Freedom is not to be equated with absence of constraint, or immunity to the accidents of natural life, or the power to dispose our fortunes as we will. The only freedom the disciples found was the freedom to do the will of God by the vanquishing of those powers within and outside themselves which had previously hindered their obedience. 'Freedom from our enemies' was one of the blessings of the promised land, as the psalmist saw it. Of course, that assumes a certain theological position. It assumes that it is of the essence of our nature to accord with and live by the inner, invisible principles of the universe. Thereby we become free; we swim with the current; we sail with the wind; we navigate by the stars; in short, we co-operate with God. We are no longer unwilling slaves to an unpredictable master, doing some incomprehensible job. We are sons, sharing our Father's concerns, entering his mind, at home in his household. The promised land to which Moses devoted his life and for which he scorned earthly delights was a land flowing with milk and honey. It was no utopia; it really existed and could have been enjoyed. The rabbis say that we shall have to give account on the last day for all the good gifts of God which we have failed to enjoy. Freedom is one of them.

There is a stream
We have been told of. Where it is
We do not know. But it is not a dream,

Though like a dream. We cannot miss
The road that leads us to it. Fate
Will take us there that keeps us here.
Neither hope nor fear
Can hasten or retard the date
Of our deliverance; when we shall leave this sand
And enter the unknown and feared and longed-for land.
(Edward Muir, *Collected Poems*, Faber & Faber.)

The freedom fighter in a totalitarian state and the
ordinary humble Christian living out his life within the
narrow confines of the 8.30 train and the swing doors
of the office have this in common – they yield to the
fascination of Edwin Muir's 'unknown and feared and
longed-for land'. It is the 'promised' land towards
which, so we believe, the whole of human history moves,
where men may live in freedom, enjoying their servitude
to God. It is another way of describing that aspiration we
express when we say, 'Thy kingdom come, thy will be
done on earth.' That kingdom is indeed in part the consequence of human effort, in so far as it is directed by the
will of God. But the Bible never altogether
surrenders the view that this kingdom is the promise of
God, the gift of God, the result of his free grace and
loving power. The freedom fighter who snatches at
freedom, for himself or for his clan, may in fact be
distancing himself from that 'unknown and feared and
longed-for land' he so eagerly desires. He may not even
see it from afar, as Moses did. It could be that the man
travelling on the 8.30 or opening his grocery store at
9.00, or the girl hammering her typewriter in the typing
pool, or the housewife laying the table for the 1,000th
time, may be winning little victories for freedom unnoticed in the world but richly treasured in heaven.
When the disciples came back excited by their little

victories over the demons, it is said that our Lord exulted in spirit and cried, 'I saw Satan as lightning fall from heaven.' In that moment the Saviour of the world glimpsed that 'unknown and feared and longed-for land' when men would be free from the tyranny of Satan, and be free indeed.

THE TOWER BLOCK

It is as true of politicians as it is of churchmen that we habitually climb on to bandwagons just when they are grinding to a halt. The church discovers the virtues of centralization just when others are beginning to experience its vices, and so it was that the Labour government came to power in 1964, on the basis of a programme geared to advanced technology and riding on a flood-tide of optimism about it. It was all about men in white coats. Not much more than a decade later the full implications of advanced technology are beginning to be felt. The dream has turned into a nightmare and a commission established by the Club of Rome felt it necessary to report that mankind had little chance of surviving beyond the year 2100 if we permitted technology to go its own unchallenged way. The commission was not concerned at that point with the ever present possibility of a nuclear holocaust, but rather with the more insidious, less dramatic effects of the extravagant use of our raw materials, the cumulative effect of environmental pollution and the social consequences of increasing automation and decreasing human control.

Alarmist? The members of this commission were sober men, possessed of as much actual information as was available, with no political axe to grind and no glib solution to offer. So we have a hundred years or so to come to terms with the limitations of growth and the dangers of a technology unduly committed to it. There is a sense in which 1964, contrary to all appearance, was not the beginning of a new technological age but the end of it. Our children could be back to subsistence farming; after us the stone age.

There is little point in taking refuge in a wholesale condemnation of technology as such; that would be to blame a delicate toy for disintegrating in clumsy hands. The brilliant technology which produced the wheel and the plough and the igloo and, more recently, the radio and penicillin and high-yield corn, has contributed immeasurably to the health and freedom of mankind. I thank God for technology every time I sit in a dentist's chair or turn on the central heating in this palace of ours or pick up the telephone and talk to our family. Even those who embrace the simple life, and get back to nature, do so in clothes made in Leeds, in cars made in Coventry, with medicines made in Widnes, and carrying old-fashioned lamps made in Hong Kong. We do not regress to the stone age as easily as we might imagine.

All the same, we have to acknowledge that something has gone seriously wrong with this particular human enterprise, as with every other human enterprise on earth. Take the tower block for example – that symbol of confidence and skill which dominates the skyline of Merseyside and many other great conurbations in the developing and developed worlds. The motives behind it were, we may suppose, unexceptionable. It was a means of housing large numbers of people under good domestic conditions within the cosy confines of a small village and at the same time with a view of the stars. It created space where otherwise, given the density of population, there would have been none. Given (as in many cases) a new industrial estate within reasonable distance of the residential area, it removed the necessity for endless travelling by the work force of the nation and reduced the mounting pressure on the roads. It enabled large new towns to be built covering a comparatively small space, with shopping facilities and cultural interests therefore close at hand.

Yet we build these giant tower blocks no more and begin to wish that we had never built them at all. They stand there, in this countryside of ours, as melancholy reminders of a well-intentioned experiment that has failed. The reasons for that failure are known to most of those who today have any responsibility for town planning or social welfare. For reasons which are by no means clear these tower blocks produce young criminals and middle-aged neurotics, disturbed families and children in need of care and attention, out of all proportion to the total numbers who inhabit them. In the days of my innocence, on a journey in the United States, I observed a very tall tower adjoining a farm complex and asked my guide what it was. It was a chicken house. The mind shuddered at the thought of tens and tens of thousands of God's creatures trapped for the duration of their natural life within those great concrete walls. I only recalled that experience when I stood, in my early days as Bishop of Liverpool, amid the tower blocks, 'vertical receptacles' as the planners used to call them.

The tower block is a sign of the times, the sign of a serious human endeavour which produced almost precisely the opposite effect to that which was intended. Of course it is possible to look at it another way. Maybe the tower block arose not simply out of genuine human concern but out of the realization that we had the technology available to build it. We can do it: therefore we must do it. The same might be said of the Concorde. Is it simply an effort to reduce the travelling time of top

16

executives and thus to hasten the wheels of business; or is it because we now have the resources to build a supersonic airliner and therefore we must build it? Everest is there: we must climb it.

The author of the book of Genesis had a comment to make upon the advanced technology of his own day – and it was a very advanced technology indeed. We still would not know how to build the pyramids or to arrange the stones at Stonehenge in a logical pattern – or to build a tower which reaches to heaven. The story of the tower of Babel is one of the most profound comments we have on the nature of the human enterprise when it ceases to be concerned with the proper dimensions of mankind and seeks to build way outside them. 'Let us build a tower which will reach to heaven.' The builders did not profess any desire to improve the lot of humankind; it was not apparent that anyone intended to occupy the tower, it was not there to house a radar beacon or to launch a satellite. It was the expression of a desire to build something which had never been built before and to build it big. It was, as the author suggests, a challenge to God. So the Lord came down to see the city and the tower and said to himself, 'This is only the beginning of what they will do and nothing that they propose to do will now be impossible to them.' It is the story of the Fall all over again. There were fruits on the tree of knowledge – why not eat them? Men could build a tower reaching to heaven – why not build it? The author was not against technology. After all the ark was a great technological achievement and he records without adverse comment that Jubal was the father of all those who play the lyre and the pipe and Tubal Cain was the forger of all instruments of bronze and iron. This Hebrew theologian had no desire to return to the wilderness, no taste for subsistence farming, no longing to divest himself of the blessings of civilization. He simply saw the dangers which we are now only beginning to perceive, of a technology which merely expresses the ambition of man, without regard for the real needs of suffering humanity. Let the new town be of such a kind that I can hear a girl laugh in the street, detect a footfall on the pavement, feel the sun on my back and the wind in my face, talk to a friend across my garden gate. Our needs are very simple; technology is a gift of God for seeing that those simple needs are met.

The author of Genesis was writing anything up to three thousand years ago. It has taken time for his precious insight into the nature of things to become vivid and urgent. It could be that we have just over a hundred years to learn the lesson and apply the remedy. Our enemies are not the town planner or the architect, the industrial magnate, or the local council. These are the stereotypes beloved of the demagogue who clothes these kindly citizens with hoof and horns and calls upon us to exorcize them. But the demagogue has his point. It could be that his stereotypes are the victims of, and unwilling allies to destructive forces always at work in men and in communities. Perhaps they do need exorcizing. It is a very striking feature of our Lord's ministry, and a singularly embarrassing one to many students of the Bible, that so much of it should have been devoted to casting out 'demons'. Was not our Lord, in this aspect at least, a child of his time? Was not demonology in any case a theological innovation of the second or third centuries BC? The revival of the black arts in our own day suggests that we may not be able to give as confident an answer as we might wish to these questions.

But demons are not necessarily decked out with horns and hoofs. They do not simply express themselves in mental disorder or group madness. They do not always take herds of pigs screaming into the deep. They may operate behind a highly respectable façade – in the board room or a union meeting. They may propose the building of a tower block or a Concorde to minds ready to receive the suggestion. Our warfare is not against flesh and blood but against principalities and powers. Technology, so the biblical authors would seem to suggest, is a gift of God for which we can only be thankful, but like so many other gifts of God it can be perverted for the aggrandizement of men. It can turn a garden into a howling desert, a community into a concentration camp, a home for heroes into a vertical receptacle.

It could be that the church ought to be less preoccupied with the symptoms of social disorder and more concerned with the causes; less ready with the palliative and more concerned for the cure; not satisfied with cooling the fevered brow but intent on finding the nature of the disorder within. The weapons of our warfare, St. Paul tells us, are mighty – to the casting down of strongholds. The followers of Jesus of Nazareth may have to take more seriously than they sometimes have their obligation to identify, resist, and cast out the demons which may well take us into the abyss – by the year 2100. We may not even live to enjoy a stone age.

It is a dangerous thing, our Lord reminded us, to cast out demons unless you have positive powers to put in their place – or else the last state will be worse than the first. Time was when the church used to build its own towers to reach heaven, reminding those who huddled beneath them that the great physical and intellectual structures of mankind must yield to the glory of God. So

19

York Minster rose in all its beauty and splendour above the squalid tenements of a medieval city, reminding the inhabitants of where they stood and what they were. The great cathedrals were an example of an advanced technology at least ostensibly devoted to the glory of God and the elevation of mankind. We can no longer rival the great secular structures around us; we do not have the resources to build even a modest tower or a short steeple. God has to be content with a *bijou* residence. So we shall have to find some other way of expressing the truth which is more consonant with the modest role the church now plays in society. By word and deed, we seek the glory and splendour of God, invite men to harness their ambitions to that one end, to submit their technology to the test of things eternal and moderate their fine schemes to fit the real needs of real men in an imperfect world. 'Tell out my soul the greatness of the Lord.'

THE DECIBEL BUSINESS

The scene is a café in a North Yorkshire country town late on a winter afternoon. There are three or four couples sitting there. Conversation is quiet and desultory. A fire is burning fitfully in the grate. Two breezy young men enter. Their conversation dies on their lips. One of them says to the girl behind the counter, 'It's quiet here ... embarrassing ... you need a radio.'

So the radio is not a source of information, or a vehicle of entertainment, but a noise-maker. No parents with teenage children will need to be told that noise is endemic to a certain kind of youth culture. It reached its deafening climax, as far as I was concerned, in the clubs of inner Liverpool, where conversation, thought, concentration, relationships, all yielded to the decibel business. No doubt it will pass – like the unkempt hair, the T-shirt, the jeans and many another fashion. Or will it pass? It would be easy to suppose that the decibel business is simply the product of a well-orchestrated advertising industry, relying for its success on electronic sound, hi-fi sets, electric guitars and radio channels entirely dominated by the disc-jockey. It is the product of unnatural groupings in university or college or club. It is the product of an era in which it is the younger wage-earners who have money to burn. But it could be that the decibel business rests on a firmer base than passing fashion or a passing economic phase. The distracted parents, who try to close their ears to the noise of stereophonic sound from the teenagers' bedroom, may be indulging their own noise mechanisms, though in a more muted, less obvious form.

The decibel business, let it be acknowledged, owes its comparatively sudden success to a combination of skilful, manipulative advertising and a technology which is able now to saturate the air almost indefinitely with noise. But no such combination would have any hope of permanent success unless, in some obscure way, it answered to the needs of society. The young man who turns the volume up wants to blot the world out – the world with its hideous past and its uncertain future, its meaningless competition and self-destructive wars, the grey uninviting world of the tarmac road and the service station. He is enveloped in sound, for a moment immune.

The unattractive world outside himself, however, is as nothing compared with the unattractive world within, of which he is only dimly but still painfully aware. What is he to make of this dark urge, this sense of meaninglessness, his failure to identify himself or to relate in any substantial way with others? What is it that is going on in the dark cells of his own mind as he struggles with his essay, or labours to finish an experiment, or picks up his coat as he knocks off from work. So, for God's sake, turn the volume up.

But is the parent in any better a position? He professes to detest the noise, as well he might, but can he bear the silence any better than his son? Any busy man will have to admit that he derives a large part of his being from being busy. When he is catching the early train or booking a seat for North America or grappling with an industrial problem or socializing with his friends, he is himself; he has an identity; he has a role; he has a significance in the world of affairs; he is the works manager, or the shop steward, or the professor, or the parish priest.

22

He is enveloped in the sound of his own multifarious activities and he is at peace. But it cannot be always so. There will be moments of languor, when nothing seems to matter any more, moments when brain and body fail him, when he lies on the beach or rests in his holiday cottage and wonders what it is all about. So back to the files and the busy round, and the old routine. Turn the volume up.

Which is the real self, we may ask – the self at home in the world of business surrounded by noise, or the self which sits at home in the silence? There is the burden of the ultimate question. Silence is not – distinctly not – always golden.

Most Holy Spirit
Burn Thou my soul
That I may turn myself within
And find Thee there
A still light
Lest rich in mine own conceit
And many plans
And wayward idlenesses
I should dread the darkness
Wherein I cannot act or plan or be self-full
That very darkness which is the light
Wherewith Thou dost envelop me
And draw me to consent
If I should only pause
And give myself to Thee

Such words evoke a warm response in the human heart, deafened by noise and overwhelmed with too much activity. But in practice, silence can be a very alarming experience. Ask the monk, or the nun, or the man in solitary confinement, or a busy parish priest on retreat, or a business man looking for a way back to reality.

Can one hear the voice of God – or even the voice of self – and live?

Once upon a time, before the Second World War, there was a regular programme on the radio fit to bear comparison with *The Archers* or *The Mousetrap* for longevity. It was called *In Town Tonight*. It opened with the sound of London traffic which was dramatically cut short by the cry *Stop!* – and then we were introduced to those in town that night. We cannot stop the traffic that way, either the traffic in the street or the traffic in our own minds. But sometimes God in his mercy provides an intermission in which another sound may be heard.

What we are accustomed to call the historical books of the Old Testament – 1 and 2 Samuel and 1 and 2 Kings – are viewed by the Hebrews themselves as 'the former prophets' for reasons which we may surmise but of which we cannot be certain. The prophets certainly figure in the books (Samuel, Nathan, Gad, Elijah, Elisha) and the books themselves bear the imprint of the prophetic view of things. According to this view, the world is not a thing-in-itself but a visible demonstration of the nature of existence as a whole. The world is a kind of burning bush for those who turn aside to see.

Nevertheless in all its outward factors that world is akin to ours. It is a world of politics and power, succession squabbles and wars, personal hardship and domestic tragedy – and it is a world in which the prophets are fully involved. Not for them the anchorite's cell or the rural retreat or the learned professor's study. They were in it up to the neck. The clash of armies, the arguments at court, confrontations and the shouting matches, constituted the decibel business of the ancient world. Even Elijah, that archetypal man of the desert, that 'Carmelite', did not hold himself aloof by any means from the political world and the council chamber. He was an activist, operating from his own deep and private place in the desert.

Yet apparently this had not entirely prepared him for the encounter with silence which he was to have at the Mount Horeb. Now in flight from the world he had dominated, he finds himself alone and stricken, faint-hearted and disillusioned, in the place of the original revelation to Israel. He hears again the voice that had been heard amidst great visible and acoustical splendour on Sinai. But he hears it now, not in the earthquake or the wind or the fire, which were his natural elements; he hears it now in 'the sound of a gentle stillness'. The busy world was hushed, the fever of life was over and his work was almost done. The author of I Kings would have us believe that it is out of the creative silence that the word comes. Wrap your face in your mantle, go out and stand at the entrance of the cave and listen for a voice. Or as Carlo Carretto puts it – 'Make some desert in your life' (in *Letters from the Desert*, D.L. & T.).

It is a long way from our town café to Horeb, yet it is a journey that everyone must make – if not willingly amidst the noise of life then unwillingly, when the noise is withdrawn, the set is dead and there is no way of turning the volume up. But the desert is a painful place full (as the Hebrews believed) of demons. You do not escape from life there, you encounter it. You may blot out the noise of the traffic in the city, but it is not so easy to blot out the traffic in your own mind. The devil waits for every son of man in the desert, ready with his temptations and his plausible quotations, his beguiling offers. Our Lord was not escaping from his vocation when he went into the desert. He was fulfilling it as the Lord and Master of the universe, in mortal combat with the evil one.

25

The church has often been seen as that which domesticates the world, making it bearable to live in, softening the hard edges, turning the jungle into a convent garden, taming the beast, repelling the demons. I thank God for the church in that role. How else would I have survived? But that is not its only role. The church remains the church in the wilderness, itself vulnerable, at risk, bewildered, afraid. But perhaps it is just at that point that it becomes capable again of hearing the voice that sounded from Sinai and may be able to offer a little sustenance to every son of man who finds himself there. For the greater part of its life, the church is the church of the great conurbation and the country town, the village and the university, embroiled in the life of the world, sometimes indistinguishable from it – but in that little café in the North Yorkshire country town there was a young man who one day will face the desert and will need the church there.

But what is the church to say to that young man in his need, or to the middle-aged business man slowly coming to terms with the reality of existence with no more worlds to conquer or new experiences to enjoy. Will it say – come to Evensong, or join our rota of sidesmen, or attend our study group, or be our treasurer? Too often indeed this is the response to an ill-expressed but deeply felt human need. So the seeker turns aside baffled, unsatisfied, and accustoms himself to his lot. But perhaps a precious opportunity has been lost, perhaps here was a soul ready for the kingdom, a life awaiting rebirth.

I thank God for the parish priest who saw in me not simply a noisy young man with a high opinion of himself, but a soul seeking and in need of new life – and pointed me not to the church, although indeed he valued it highly, but to Christ. Sometimes the church is admittedly every bit as deafening and distracting in its multifarious activities as the hi-fi, or the city office. Men in their deepest need do not need more activities, even ecclesiastical ones; they need to come to the point of self-knowledge and self-surrender. The point is made in an unexpected way in chapter 1 of St. Mark's gospel. I say 'unexpected' because we are not always as aware as we ought to be of the mordant irony which sometimes informs Hebrew literature in general and the gospels in particular.

St. Mark has described what we must take to be a typical ministerial day in our Lord's life. He had called his first four disciples, he had taught in the synagogue, cast out an unclean spirit, healed Simon's mother-in-law. 'In the evening when the sun set they brought unto him all that were sick and them that were possessed with devils and all the city was gathered together at the door. And he healed many that were sick with various diseases and cast out many devils.' Like so many gospel passages it can pass through the mind without leaving any permanent record there until the reader appreciates the fact that it was the sabbath day which ends, in accordance with Hebrew custom, at six o'clock in the evening when the sun sets.

So Mark is saying that when the synagogue services were over and the people had had their fill of singing psalms and hearing sermons, when the sacred scrolls had been put away in the cupboard and the collection had been counted and the synagogue door shut, then it was that the people in their real needs gathered round the door of a real healer. What the church in its multifarious activities had failed to do Christ, the son of a carpenter, did. The new Israel, as the old, will have to

27

learn to accept the judgement on itself that it often palpably fails to minister to its members or would-be members in anything but their most superficial needs. The hungry sheep look up and are not fed, the hungry teenager, the hungry business man, the hungry don, the hungry football fan, the hungry housewife on the seventh floor.

An experienced evangelist once said to me that at the end of an interview he was apt to say, 'Is there anything else you want to say to me?' Behind the superficial problems within the noisy chamber of a man's heart there is often another voice speaking which he himself scarcely identifies, summoning him to self-knowledge and self-surrender. But at some point there must be someone to embolden him to let the voice be heard.

A very striking book was published in the early part of the Second World War under the pen name Nicodemus, entitled *Midnight Hour*. It was the journal of a distinguished, highly-cultivated man struggling with the dread fact of human existence and for the first time in his life determined to win. This is how he puts it:

This journal is thus the deliberate record, made originally for myself alone, of this effort towards a complete awareness of our situation, of a 'full look at the Worst' and of a descent below all the political, ethical and spiritual patterns of our life which seemed to be daily disintegrating before my eyes, to the 'great waters' of the underworld of our consciousness in the vague and vain hope that I might remould my own cosmos from my own chaos ... It was during the next three months that the real conflict was engaged and consummated; by the end of July I had been granted an unpredictable peace. The remainder of the journal printed here for August and September records not conflict, but the gradually unfolding vision of a reconceived Christianity as seen from that 'Still Centre'.

I read that book as a young man in the Royal Air Force and was deeply moved by it, seeking to discover for myself that same 'still centre' which Christianity, as I understood it, had done so much to obscure. Many years later I met the author by then in the grip of terminal cancer. He knew his end was near and he was at peace. Is there anything else the church can offer to compare with that precious gift? The young man in the café needs it – and his friend behind the counter.

'There comes a midnight hour,' Kierkegaard said, 'when all men must unmask' (*Kierkegaard Anthology*, Oxford). It was this sentence which gave rise to the title *Midnight Hour* and to the pen name Nicodemus. For Nicodemus was inextricably involved with the religion of his forefathers, an expert, learned and serious. Many poets have tried to do justice to this particular narrative in St. John's gospel. Here is one such effort by Clive Sansom in his book *The Witnesses* (Methuen):

Then one day – it was Passover time –
Hearing tales of this travelling preacher,
I dared my orthodoxy to the point of listening.
He was a young man, barely thirty,
Formerly a carpenter, they said, from the north country,
Though with his plain tunic and plainer speech
It was hard to place him. Instantly I knew –
Young as he was, old and confirmed as I –
He held some knowledge, some instinctive truth,
That one who read himself blind on occasions
Never possessed: the very core of life.
Impossible for me, a member of the Sanhedrin,
Intellectually omnipotent to address him there –
The respectable tortoise must respect his shell!
But I spoke to a disciple – John, I think –
And arranged a meeting later in his lodgings.
It was a clear night – the Passover moon,

29

And a strong wind blowing. Concealing myself
Under my cloak, drawing it around my face –
A precaution against the wind, I assured myself –
I followed him down a labyrinth of streets
Till I found myself standing by an upper window
In full moonlight, high above the city,
The white light burnished on the temple roof.
'It is he, master – Nicodemus ...'
I saw him watch my wrinkled neck emerge,
And knew he knew me. 'You,' I began,
Hiding beneath words, 'are a teacher sent from God.'
It was difficult to continue, wanting knowledge
And afraid of knowledge. He read my silence.
'No man can reach the Kingdom by thought alone:
He must be re-born in the spirit.'
He spoke to a part of me I had often silenced,
Fearing the consequences of its rashness.
I sought my shell again, feigning stupidity.
'How, master, can a man have two births?'
He: 'Unless the spirit conceives in him,
The Kingdom will never come.'
Another silence. Only the cool night wind
Rustling my silken robe, stirring the trees.

This for Nicodemus was the midnight hour when all men
must unmask, and in the silence he struggled with the
deepest issues of his life. The poem goes on to describe his
timorous withdrawal from the struggle and ends with
these words:

Only, some evenings, when the night wind blows,
My spirit stirs again, and I remember.

Clive Sansom left it there, but thank God the author of
the fourth gospel gave the story a happier ending, and
Nicodemus associated himself publicly with Christ:
'Nicodemus brought with him a mixture of myrrh and
aloes more than half a hundredweight. They took the

body of Jesus and wrapped it, with the spices, in strips of linen cloth according to Jewish burial customs. Now at the place where he had been crucified there was a garden, and in the garden a new tomb, not yet used for burial. There, because the tomb was near at hand and it was the eve of the Jewish Sabbath, they laid Jesus.' Andrew Young thus describes the scene in his poetic drama *Nicodemus* (in *Collected Poems*, Rupert Hart Davis):

> I came tonight to speak to your dead body,
> To touch it with my hands and say 'Forgive',
> For though I knew it could not speak to me
> Or even hear, yet it was once yourself;
> It is dissolved and risen like a dew,
> And now I know,
> As dawn forgives the night, as spring the winter,
> You have forgiven me. It is enough.
> Why do I kneel before your empty tomb?
> You are not here, for you are everywhere;
> The grass, the trees, the air, the wind, the sky,
> Nothing can now refuse to be your home;
> Nor I. Lord live in me and I shall live.
> This is the word you spoke,
> The whole earth hears it, for the whole earth cries,
> *I am the resurrection, and the life; he that believeth in me though*
> *he were dead, yet shall he live: and whosoever liveth and believeth*
> *in me shall never die.*

The café on the North Yorkshire moors is not so far as we might suppose from Jerusalem in the first century. There are only two ways of coping with the human condition – we either turn the volume up, drown ourselves in noise and activity, or we dare to risk the silence, the self, the Christ. 'When the night wind blows, my spirit stirs again, and I remember.'

31

THE YOUNG VANDAL

> A successful raid in 455 resulted in the brief capture of Rome which was plundered. Gaiseric's successors were weaker men and Vandals, being Arians, remained estranged from their Catholic subjects. In 533 the Byzantine General Belisarius overthrew their last king Gelimer in a brief campaign, and the Vandals vanished from history. (*Dictionary of World History*, Nelson.)

The learned historian is of course right, but he might have put it another way if he had ever walked through a Liverpool street on a Sunday morning after the night before; or followed in the wake of the supporters of a defeated away side; or observed the hideous ineffaceable graffiti on a shining new building. The vandals are still with us – and young vandals at that, with a long career of vandalism ahead of them. We have begun to build churches without windows. Vandalism is a very troublesome phenomenon. It obtrudes upon us; it leaves glass in the streets; it makes telephone boxes inoperable and causes people to die for lack of immediate medical help. It is present, though in a lesser degree, in a small town, as well as in the large, and young children move straight from breaking toys to breaking bones. Reactions to it vary: bring back the birch; put more policemen on the beat; execrate the school teacher; fine the parents; write an indignant letter to the Times; or even, mobilize it in the cause of anarchy. It must be obvious, however, that the cause, and therefore the cure, lies much deeper than these instant remedies would suggest. What is the modern vandal saying to the world?

The vandal is very much the product of the affluent society which boasts of a superabundance of things. I was brought up in the Forest of Dean – as beautiful then as it is now, but then a depressed area. We did not have vandalism; we could not afford it – a kitchen chair had to last a thousand years. But perhaps it is not the abundance of goods alone but the attitude towards them which drives the young vandal on to the streets.

Vandalism is an unconscious protest against materialism – that attitude to life which expresses itself in glossy homes and clinical towns, in packaged pleasure and supermarkets, in concrete play areas and professionalized welfare. So the vandal rises up and cries *Destroy! Destroy!* Why sit in front of the television in a stuffy sitting-room watching destructive processes at work when you can be out on the street doing it yourself? He has no means of being or feeling significant in such a world. He will never own a yacht or have a cocktail cabinet; he will never fly in a Concorde or receive an honorary degree; he will never create a work of art or be asked to choose his 'Desert Island Discs'; but he has it in his power to destroy those material things to which this particular society attaches such inordinate importance. The more impressive the artefact the more likely it is to suffer at the hands of the vandal. They sacked Rome – now it is Birmingham and New York and Peking. We are all in it together – the universal problem of a civilization almost totally devoted to things, be it Marxist or capitalist.

For every vandal on the football terrace or in the down-town café, there are a thousand crypto-vandals. They sit behind office desks; they read good books in charming homes; they ride out on a Sunday to the golf club; they adorn the senior common room and are kind to their children. But within them, as within every son of man, there is a kind of rage – not against society (for they are well adjusted to it) but simply against things-as-they-are. The rage which the vandal expresses in the streets, the musician expresses in unmusical music, the artist in anarchic art, the dramatist in kitchen-sink drama, the satirist in sick humour. There is a kind of nihilism abroad which both reflects and is reflected in what is being increasingly seen as a wholly inadequate view of life.

We have grown accustomed to the idea that every problem can be solved; that every illness can be cured; that all protagonists can be reconciled; that death can be indefinitely deferred; that work can be made pleasurable; that things will get better and better. I remember a conference in Oxford, at which a book by a nineteenth-century secular humanist was quoted. I derived some hope from the fact that the conference members rolled in the aisles at the thought that less than a hundred years ago anyone could believe it. I derive some hope, because there is no hope for a civilization which continues to pin its aspirations on such a view of life. The human condition is beset with ambiguity, weakness and sin. There is no neatly packaged commodity called 'happiness' available for us in the super-stores of the east or of the west, of the north or of the south. The serious earthquakes in China in 1976 provoked a curious political, as well as human crisis, as if somehow earthquakes ought not to happen in a Marxist society. They challenged, in an uncomfortable way, the omni-competence of the modern state; they were an affront to a view of life which does not take the human condition seriously.

34

There is nothing new about vandalism except the particular form it happens to take in our own day. It is an expression of rage and it has, perhaps unexpectedly, its counterpart within the pages of holy scripture. Job was a good family man, well adjusted to life, secure in his possessions and a godly man withal. The terrible things in life always happened to other people. As Satan said, there was a hedge around him and around his house and around all that he had. But war, fire, hurricane and disease changed all that, and at last Job experienced to the full the exigencies of the human condition – pain, physical and mental isolation and, worst of all, the 'comforters'. Alas for the comforters of mankind who cry *Peace! Peace!* when there is no peace, and heal the wounds of the people lightly. They had all kinds of solutions which they pressed with increasing fervour upon the unhappy Job. They would have been amongst the phalanx who would bring back the birch; or increase the size of the police force; or write letters to the Times; or build churches without windows. But their solutions were just fuel to Job's rage: 'What a fine help you are to me, poor weak man that I am. You give such good advice and share your knowledge with a fool like me. Who do you think will hear all your words? Who inspired you to speak like this?' The fact of the matter is that there are no solutions.

No solutions? That would be unfair to the book of Job. There may be no 'solutions' but there is a 'resolution'. The sufferings through which Job passes issue in an experience of God within which life takes on a new aspect. Job is not thereby delivered from the human condition but he is delivered from rage against it. He sees the world now, and himself within it, as under the overarching, all-wise providence of a loving creator. He is a different person, content to live with mysteries. 'I talked about things I did not understand; about marvels too great for me to know. You told me to listen while you spoke and to try to answer your questions, then I knew only what others had told me but now I have seen you with my own eyes, so I am ashamed of all I have said and repent in dust and ashes.' After that the author rather quaintly says, Job lived a hundred and forty years. He deserved to!

We may have to build churches without windows to foil the vandals and to appease the insurers. You cannot break into a church so easily if it has no windows; but then you cannot see out so clearly either. The church is not here to offer easy solutions to insoluble problems. Job's comforters were well-meaning, highly sympathetic, zealous and orthodox individuals, but they entirely failed the man they sought to serve. The church witnesses to a man who faced the rigours of existence, who did not turn aside from pain, and who plumbed the depths of isolation and meaninglessness. They vandalized him on the cross. He did not attempt to heal the wounds of his people lightly. He did not say, 'Peace, peace.' He said, with a confidence based upon his own experience, that in the world we would have tribulation. But he also said, 'I have overcome the world.' He was perfectly adapted to life as it is, not to some unimaginable life to which the reactionary calls us back and to which the revolutionary calls us forward. There was no rage in him.

The vandals, like the poor, are with us always. They do not 'vanish from history'; they are a challenge to the world beset with untruths. They are a challenge to the church entrusted with the truth, for no better reason than that someone must be entrusted with it.

But what is the truth with which the church is entrusted? The young vandal is not alone. We have seen that he has his counterparts in the worlds of literature, music and art. Take for example this quotation from Baxandall's *Radical Perspectives in the Arts* (Penguin):

Ugliness was for the Naturalists in modern times similar to the sublime and the tragic, above all a protest against the beautiful, against its claim to exclusiveness within the realm of art. The Dadaists and Surrealists preferred the ugly in the name of life, of a new try at the social order, of an imagination which respects neither dogma nor boundary. The way led forward from Dadaism to provocative spectacles such as Yves Klein arranged in Paris. When his model climbed into a tub of blue paint, then impressed her 'pose' on a white canvas, there was more than moral scandal involved. Here was the destructive gesture of an artist whose intention evoked an illusion, the better to unmask illusionism in art. In Rauschenberg's work of 1962, The Bed, what one sees is the artist's own blanket and pillow which he has sprayed with colour. Here is at once a furtherance of the Dadaist protest against aestheticism, and the mockery of a civilization in which possessions are everything. In a differing yet kindred creative mode is the work of Hasior, a Pole who emphasizes the banality of the object – old rubbish receives treatment as an interesting material – which he goes on to ornament with plebeian motifs derived from folklore. Ugliness is here given a symbolic sense owing to the tradition to which the artist relates and which he at the same time deconsecrates.

Deconsecrates is the significant word. We in the west are the product of two related but often competing cultures – Hebraic and Hellenic. Both of them in their way express in varying modes the belief that the world is orderly, beautiful, significant. The Hebraic tradition goes infinitely further than the Hellenic by insisting not only that the world is orderly, beautiful and significant, but that it owes all these attributes to the activity of a loving creator. The Bible everywhere rings with this abiding truth, but nowhere more exultantly than in Psalm 104. I quote from the Good News Bible (Bible Societies/Collins):

Praise the Lord, my soul!
O Lord, my God, how great you are!
You are clothed with majesty and glory;
you cover yourself with light.
You spread out the heavens like a tent
and built your home on the waters above.
You use the clouds as your chariot
and ride on the wings of the wind.
You use the winds as your messengers
and flashes of lightning as your servants.

You have set the earth firmly on its foundations
and it will never be moved.
You placed the ocean over it like a robe,
and the water covered the mountains.
When you rebuked the waters, they fled;
they rushed away when they heard your shout of command.
They flowed over the mountains and into the valleys,
to the place you had made for them.
You set a boundary they can never pass,
to keep them from covering the earth again.

You make springs flow in the valleys,
and rivers run between the hills.
They provide water for the wild animals;
there the wild donkeys quench their thirst.
In the trees near by,
the birds make their nests and sing.

From the sky you send rain on the hills,
and the earth is filled with your blessings.
You make grass grow for the cattle
and plants for man to use,
so that he can grow his crops
and produce wine to make him happy,
olive-oil to make him cheerful,
and bread to give him strength.

The cedars of Lebanon get plenty of rain –
the Lord's own trees, which he planted.
There the birds build their nests;
the storks nest in the fir-trees.
The wild goats live in the high mountains,
and the badgers hide in the cliffs.

You created the moon to mark the months;
the sun knows the time to set.
You made the night, and in the darkness
all the wild animals come out.
The young lions roar while they hunt,
looking for the food that God provides.
When the sun rises, they go back
and lie down in their dens.
Then people go out to do their work
and keep working until evening.

Lord, you have made so many things!
How wisely you made them all!
The earth is filled with your creatures.

Within the context of such a world view vandalism is
unthinkable unless it be the mischievous vandalism of a
Samson destroying his enemies' crops by fire. The trees
are the creation of God, not of the parks and gardens
department; cats reflect the glory of God, and are not
to be clubbed to death for fun; farms are God's provision
for our needs, not to be trampled over by reckless

holidaymakers in pursuit of pleasure. But more than that, they are all part of a coherent meaningful system – infinitely sensitive, in which the sun rises and sets, and the rains come and the winds blow – to be treated with reverence and awe. Yes, *deconsecrates* is the significant word. We live now in the wash of a philosophical system which banished God from the world of things, leaving room indeed for the private religion, a religion of self-culture, a religion of withdrawal, but leaving no room for the grand Hebraic conception of the universe as the domain of a loving providence. Atheism leads on to vandalism.

The young vandal has to live in a world created by the culture and values of the society to which he belongs. He is the victim of other people's atheism. We have deconsecrated the world. Why should he revere it? Who but the philosopher (or a vandal) could survive in the atheist's world as it is described for us by Bertrand Russell in his book *Why I am not a Christian* (National Secular Society):

> Brief and powerless is man's life; on him and all his race the slow, sure doom falls pitiless and dark. Blind to good and evil, reckless of destruction, omnipotent matter rolls on its relentless way; for man, condemned today to lose his dearest, tomorrow himself to pass through the gate of darkness, it remains only to cherish, ere yet the blow fall, the lofty thoughts that ennoble his little day; disdaining the coward terrors of the slave of Fate, to worship at the shrine that his own hands have built; undismayed by the empire of chance, to preserve a mind free from the wanton tyranny that rules his outward life; proudly defiant of the irresistible forces that tolerate, for a moment, his knowledge and his condemnation, to sustain, alone, a weary but unyielding Atlas, the world that his own ideals have fashioned despite the trampling march of unconscious power.

You have to be a very old philosopher or a very young vandal to live in such a world.

With this world-view compare that of another philosopher, the author of Ecclesiastes:

> The Words of the Speaker, the son of David, king in Jerusalem.
>
> Emptiness, emptiness, says the Speaker, emptiness, all is empty. What does man gain from all his labour and his toil here under the sun? Generations come and generations go, while the earth endures for ever. The sun rises and the sun goes down; back it returns to its place and rises there again. The wind blows south, the wind blows north, round and round it goes and returns full circle. All streams run into the sea, yet the sea never overflows; back to the place from which the streams ran they return to run again.
>
> All things are wearisome; no man can speak of them all. Is not the eye surfeited with seeing, and the ear sated with hearing? What has happened will happen again, and what has been done will be done again, and there is nothing new under the sun. (Ecclesiastes 1:1–9, New English Bible.)

But somehow even this cynical observer of human affairs could not entirely extinguish the faith of his fathers. His mind was dominated by the endless succession of natural events empty, so he believed, of meaning. Yet he could never entirely deconsecrate the world. 'He has given men a sense of time past and future, but no comprehension of God's work from beginning to end.' No comprehension – but he did not deduce from that that there was nothing to comprehend. Along the pulses he sensed the truth, and his urbane reductionist view of things yields in the end to the basic conviction which his own bitter experience of life was not able entirely to destroy – 'Remember your Creator in the days of your youth' ... yes, in the days of your youth.

41

THE DEPARTURE LOUNGE

So here I sit in the departure lounge awaiting the final call. My few possessions wanted 'on voyage' are around me. Times without number I have checked that I have airline tickets, my passport, my vaccination certificate, my visa, my foreign money, my travellers cheques. I have a large book as a hedge against boredom. I have had three cups of coffee. I have padded fruitlessly round the duty-free shop. I have studied the provisons provided by a friendly insurance company – £5,000 for the loss of one arm; £10,000 for the loss of two; £15,000 for the loss of two arms and a leg ... And I am just in the right frame of mind to welcome the announcement that the departure has been delayed because of a technical fault. Nevertheless, in due course, I shall find myself encapsulated in a cabin. I shall observe the notice over my head which says that passengers are not to be alarmed if they see blue flames coming out of the engine because, in this particular aircraft, that is normal. I shall listen to the voice and watch the demonstrator as, for the ten thousandth time, she explains what we are to do in the event of disaster. I view the emergency exits without enthusiasm and think of my days in the RAF when it was so much simpler – you just turned the thing upside-down and fell out. But there is soothing music, of the kind they presumably play to battery hens, and soon the little tables will be coming down in front of us to remind us again of that unfortunate analogy. There is ten-tenths cloud underneath us and we are flying west, keeping up with the sun but seeing absolutely nothing except those endless fleecy clouds underneath and the unbroken blue sky above. We shall touch down all right; the crew is competent, the navigation impeccable. And we shall be in the new world, the other side of the Jordan.

Meanwhile I sit in the departure lounge awaiting the final call, and from my upholstered chair I view humanity circling endlessly around me – anxious, bored, preoccupied. The departure lounge is a sign of the times, giving in its own way a peculiar emphasis to certain features of our humanity which are otherwise obscured from us. The departure lounge is a first sign of crowds without community. I am surrounded by people but am absolutely alone, trapped in that little circle of floor space which contains me and my possessions. Even if I were able to identify someone I knew, he too would be trapped in his floor space with a different destination in view and a different objective. We would converse and pass, he on his errand and I on mine. The only thing we have in common is that we happen to be in the same departure lounge at the same time. He will hurry off at his final call and I will hurry off at mine. Were there twenty thousand people in the departure lounge, it would be the same – or a hundred thousand or a thousand million.

One of the great new factors on the human scene is the giant conurbation. City culture is of course as old as Babylon or Thebes, Alexandria or Rome, but the greater part of mankind lived out their lives in the fields and the forests, largely unaffected by the great cities of the world which they knew only by hearsay. But now it is said more than two thirds of the United Kingdom's population lives either within, or within the purlieus of one of the great cities. In Australia, that place of huge open spaces and of tough pioneers, the proportion is even higher. We are in danger of being part of one giant conurbation, pressed closer and closer together, with no better reason for being together than that that is how it just happens to be. The sewage system, the electricity grid, leisure and shopping facilities require that it should be so.

It is a myth, widely propagated, that the church is traditionally more successful in the country than in the town. In the short perspectives of western history, that is no doubt so. But the church in its early days achieved its most spectacular successes in the cities of the ancient world. It was in the *pagus* (the country) that the pagan was to be found. This is hardly surprising, given the antecedents of the church. The Jews had become essentially an urban people, carrying on their trades, engaging in commerce, art and government in the cities. It was no mean task for the zionists to persuade the founders of the kibbutz movement to try their hand at husbandry. Have you ever met a Jewish farmer?

It was inevitable, therefore, that the propagation of the gospel should be most effective in the towns where communities of Jews and godfearers were already to be found. The church followed the synagogue into the inner city areas and new towns of the Roman empire. We must, at least in part, attribute the success of the early church to the fact that it found a place in already existing communities, bound together by a common attitude to life, a common faith, a common sacred book, a common code of conduct. It may be that the future of the church in this country will depend less upon its ability to ape the structures of the secular world and more upon its sheer distinction from them.

44

Man cannot live for ever in a departure lounge. Short of that far off state, in which we recognize a common humanity and live together on the basis of it, we shall have to be content to be members of groups, bound together in some common cause or by some common interest, or in pursuit of some common objective. The homelessness of man offers the church an opportunity, not simply of increasing its membership but of ministering to the deepest needs of man in the communities where Christians live. God is our father and all we are brothers – not just names on a boarding list.

The departure lounge holds up a mirror also to another feature of contemporary life, made more painful by our sudden awareness of it. The departure lounge stands for activity without purpose. There is in fact nothing to do, but we are uncommonly busy doing it, buying useless objects in the airport shop, drinking unnecessary cups of coffee in the airport café, listening unnecessarily to announcements, with our flight still an hour or so ahead. We fret. I sometimes wonder as I go on some of my 'unnecessary' journeys down the motorway or across the province – where is everyone else going and why? My objectives are clear enough to me, I think, but how will they look when seen with hindsight from the retirement cottage and the occasional duty and the empty in-tray? What then of my projects, my speeches, my working lunches, my pamphlets, letters and books? 'I have seen all the works that are done under the sun,' says the wise man of Israel, 'and behold, all is vanity and a striving after wind.' I await the final call. It is understandable, perhaps inevitable, that the church should be caught up in the intense activism of twentieth-century civilization, where everything appears to depend upon us, and infinitely complex schemes for the present and the future engage our energies. But perhaps the time will come when the church will have to be content to *be* rather than to *do*, to provide a place, as P. T. Forsyth puts it, 'up there in the hills where He can show us transfigured things in a noble light, within a fellowship, gracious, warm and noble' (*Spirit of Prayer*, Independent Press).

The gospels, on the whole, are notably quiet about the things we are required to do but persistent on what we ought to be. The Lord of life himself did not entirely yield to the clamour of the cities. So the author of the second epistle of Peter, trapped (as he felt himself to be) in a phrenetic, disintegrating world, has this to say to the church of his day: 'Since the whole universe is to break up in this way, think what sort of people you ought to be, what devout and dedicated lives you should live . . . with this to look forward to, do your utmost to be found at peace with him, unblemished and above reproach in his sight.' The church which is content to be, will have a powerful attraction for those who have grown disillusioned with trying to do.

Above all, perhaps, the departure lounge stands for endless precautions without enduring security. There is a sense, of course, in which the lavish insurance arrangements which are on offer do provide a kind of security – without arms or legs. It is true that the life jacket under your seat will keep you afloat in the freezing waters of the mid-Atlantic for several hours. It is true that blue flames do come out of the engine without necessarily setting the aeroplane alight. But the sky is very large and the sea is very deep. Pilots have their fatal moments of inattention and sophisticated electronic devices sometimes fail. Security is everywhere promised in this world and is never to be found. The insurance man and the safety inspectors, the road engineer and the motor mechanic are no match for the exigencies of the human condition. The final call does come and we head out into the blue, on an unknown journey, taking little with us. We go on hoodwinking ourselves, most of us, with our health regimes and our strict diets and our insurance policies and our pensions, because we cannot bear too much reality.

The Son of Man, our Lord says – and he is not simply speaking for himself but for every son of man – has nowhere to lay his head; he is much, much less secure than the fox and the bird. Here we have no continuing city. It is therefore perhaps more important for the church to make the next world real, than just to make this world bearable. We must question that attitude of mind, powerful even in the church, which silently assumes that man can live by bread alone and that the vocation of the clergyman, in order to be real, must be concerned with the little securities that men crave for. There are, of course, the little securities which we all enjoy, but they are enjoyed as passengers enjoy their little securities in a metal aircraft, air-conditioned, with attentive air-hostesses and regular meals and a life-jacket under the seat. It still remains true that the sky is infinite and the sea is deep. Somehow or other, the church of God must provide a home for the son of man in what is otherwise a totally mysterious and ultimately threatening universe. 'This is eternal life,' St. John said, 'that you should believe in him whom God has sent.' For myself, I know of no other security in heaven or on earth. He is the rock on whom I build, the refuge in whom I hide, the way, the truth, the life.

Passengers on flight B14 are asked to go at once to Gate 23. Please have your boarding pass ready. So I pick up my few possessions, clutch the book which I have only pretended to read and join a motley of people whom I have never seen before and am likely never to see again, and make my way past gates number 1, 2, 3 ... 13, 14 ... 19, 20. Above me the sky, below me the sea. In the words of the psalmist (Psalm 139): 'If I ascend up into heaven, thou art there: if I make my bed in hell, behold, thou art there. If I take the wings of the morning, and dwell in the uttermost parts of the sea; Even there shall thy hand lead me, and thy right hand shall hold me. If I say, Surely the darkness shall cover me; even the night shall be light about me. Yea, the darkness hideth not from thee; but the night shineth as the day: the darkness and the light are both alike to thee.'

Within the pulseless solitude
Between the pebble and the star,
Where flesh can live not, though it would
The spirit's stubborn anchors are.

THE NEWS READER

Across the screens of a thousand million living-rooms flicker the familiar images of ritual violence, political confrontation, show business, trendy drama, long-running domestic serials, cops and robbers, cowboys and Indians and all the stars in their courses. But amidst them all, I ask you to observe – the news reader. Elegantly dressed with a dash of informality, young enough to be appealing, old enough to be dignified, presenting a shrewd mixture of authority, reliability, compassion and humour. He has been carefully chosen; he is an important figure in the news industry.

The news industry is one of the signs of our time. Forests are denuded every month to provide the newsprint. Thousands of feet of film are used every day to provide us with pictures of the latest outrage, or this evening's match in Europe, or the picket lines in some unhappy industry. The world is a network of electronic communication, with space satellites as the latest element in it. Journalists, printers, editors, camera men, interviewers, producers, directors, ticker-tape operators, all go to make up one of the biggest industries of the modern world. Every hour on the radio, several times a day on the television, and at least twice a day in the newspapers you may encounter, if you wish, the same bad news.

But perhaps it would be safer to say that this massive news industry is distinctive of our times only in its size and its complexity. Men have always hungered for news. In one of the oldest documents available to us it is told how

Eli sat upon his seat by the wayside watching and waiting, for his heart trembled for the Ark of God ... What is the news my son?

And this is from the same book, with David waiting in a fever of apprehension for the news of the battle against his rebellious son Absalom:

David was sitting between the two gates when the watchman went up to the roof of the gatehouse by the wall and, looking out, saw a man running alone. The watchman called to the king and told him. 'If he is alone,' said the king, 'then he has news.' The man came nearer and nearer. Then the watchman saw another man running. He called down to the gate-keeper and said, 'Look, there is another man running alone.' The king said, 'He too brings news.' The watchman said, 'I see by the way he runs that the first runner is Ahimaaz son of Zadok.' The king said, 'He is a good fellow and shall earn the reward for good news.' Ahimaaz called out to the king, 'All is well!' He bowed low before him and said, 'Blessed be the Lord your God who has given into your hands the men who rebelled against your majesty.' The king asked, 'Is all well with the young man Absalom?' Ahimaaz answered, 'Sir, your servant Joab sent me, I saw a great commotion, but I did not know what had happened.' The king told him to stand to one side; so he turned aside and stood there. Then the Cushite came in and said, 'Good news, your majesty! The Lord has avenged you this day on all those who rebelled against you.' The king said to the Cushite, 'Is all well with the young man Absalom?' The Cushite answered, 'May all the king's enemies and all rebels who would do you harm be as that young man is.' The king was deeply moved and went up to the roof-chamber over the gate and wept, crying out as he went, 'O, my son! Absalom my son, my son Absalom! If only I had died instead of you! O Absalom, my son, my son.' (2 Samuel 18:24–33, New English Bible.)

We may not be able to match this heart-rending prose from one of the great literary monuments of the Old Testament but we all know what it feels like to hunger for and at the same time to dread the arrival of news. So Nehemiah, a Jew exiled in Babylon, but still devoted to Jerusalem the city of his fathers, sat down and wept and mourned for many days when he heard that the wall of Jerusalem was broken down and the gates had been destroyed by fire.

But these are examples of highly personalized news, news to provoke the joy or the grief of those who receive it. The ancient world knew nothing of what we now call the 'mass media', which is as much a branch of entertainment as it is of information – to be mulled over, commented on, and interpreted for the benefit of those who have a spare hour every morning in the train, or a long drive down the motorway, or a boring evening in the hotel room. The news may be either good or bad but at all costs it must be interesting; it must command the attention; it must provoke excitement.

The news reader occupies a more important place in the broadcasting hierarchy than we might suppose. His task is infinitely more difficult than the inveterate news watcher might imagine. He dominates the screen for as much as half an hour at a time, preparing his audience for the pictures that are about to appear, commenting upon them after they appear. He has to give a certain sense of continuity and, ideally, a sense of balance – emphasizing the important, passing lightly over the unimportant. He must achieve the right sense of solemnity when the news calls for it. He has, if possible, to end on a cheerful note with a smiling goodnight and 'See you tomorrow'. Woe betide the news reader who smiles at the wrong place or gives an unfortunate edge to an item of news with an unseemly lift of the eyebrows. He has a wider public than any other single performer on television. He is infinitely better known than any news editor and certainly than any newspaper proprietor. He is recognized in the street when a cabinet minister may pass unnoticed. His departure or promotion has to be carefully prepared by the television authorities because of the gap he will leave in the living room of No. 3 Acacia Road or in the drawing room of a stately home.

I ask myself why this should be so, and I conclude that it is because he provides a reassuring presence amidst the devastations surrounding him. An apartment house is blown-up in Belfast; there are pictures of hijacked passengers shivering in a plane; a widow bowed down with grief at the loss of her husband; children being rescued from flooded streets; villagers picking up the pieces after a violent tornado; soldiers wounded and dying in some outpost war. How can this be made bearable to mortal man without the reassuring presence, the cultured voice and the assurance that he will see you tomorrow? He will be there when the end comes, when 'the sun will be darkened and the moon will not give her light, the stars will fall from the sky, celestial powers will be shaken.' He will be there in his familiar seat when the air is full of dust and the walls collapse around him. In this world of dangerous disturbances, universally disseminated by the mass media, he is essential. Thank God for that reassuring presence.

The news reader is at the same time a symbol both of our hunger for news and of the dread which answers to it. For the greater part we are observers rather than participants. It is unlikely that our house will ever be blown up or that we would be passengers in a hijacked aircraft or that we shall die in some green jungle far away. There is a sense in which civilization protects us from these hideous events in ourselves and exposes us to them in the lives of others. This, far more than the ritual violence or the obscene utterance, may constitute the real danger of television. It has after all been known for people to suppose that a bank robbery is being staged for the sake of the television cameras and therefore to withhold their aid from real policemen struggling with real robbers and suffering from real wounds. We live vicariously rather than dangerously.

But for the greater part of mankind's history, men have had to endure the slings and arrows of outrageous fortune, unprotected by a friendly welfare state, suffering in their own bodies the ravages of battle or disease, seeing their homes torn down by marauders, watching their crops burnt by invading armies, dying at home and not in the hospital, watching their children slaughtered before their eyes, and dreading the night. They needed a reassuring presence to cope with their own troubles, not just with the vicarious experience of other peoples troubles. They needed a wise interpreter of the chiaroscuro of life which passed before their eyes. They needed the priest, representing the timeless traditions of their race, offering the sacrifices with the enemy at the gate, back again at the reconstructed altar when the enemy passed and life resumed its normal course. They needed the prophet with his secret knowledge of the ways of God, able to perceive light at the end of the tunnel, to observe the hand of God in the bleak and deadly experiences of everyday life. Priest and prophet were the representatives of the eternal and the permanent, of the abiding and the real, amidst the confusions of personal and national history.

So perhaps all we have done is to substitute the news reader, seemingly wise and sympathetic, for the priest and the prophet – without any essential loss. We find the illusion of permanence essential and we find it in him.

But that may not be the whole story. The priests and the prophets were not, with some unhappy exceptions, illusionists. They really believed in the permanent and the real and the eternal, and they consistently sought to lead their devotees on to a similar belief. They were not employees in an entertainment industry but the servants of the living God.

It is striking that the contents of the New Testament should be broadly comprehended under the term *gospel*, that is to say, they are to be understood not as dogma, information, history, or philosophy, but as news, and always with the affirmative prefix – *good* news. But is there, for heaven's sake, any good news, or do we have to be content to lurch from one crisis to the next; emerge out of one disaster to be swallowed by another? Will it be 'as when a man runs from a lion, and a bear meets him, or turns into a house and leans his hand on the wall, and a snake bites him' (Amos 5:19, New English Bible)? Perhaps the day of the Lord is indeed 'darkness, not light, a day of gloom with no dawn' (verse 20). To that question the New Testament (and with slightly less confidence the Old Testament) gives a resounding *no*. 'Seek the Lord,' said that same prophet Amos, 'and you shall live ... Seek him that maketh the seven stars and Orion, and turneth the shadow of death into the morning, and maketh the day dark with night: that calleth for the waters of the sea, and poureth them out upon the face of the earth: The Lord is his name.' (Amos 5:6, 8, Authorized Version.)

But in the life and teaching of Jesus the good news

takes a more positive form, achieving a grandeur and a depth which is, as far as my knowledge goes, unique in the history of religion. He is everywhere conscious of living in a savage world, where towers fall on innocent people and wars ravage the countryside and sparrows lie dying in the gutter, but at the same time overwhelmingly conscious of the unfailing love of God and the permanence of his kingdom. He could have sat in front of the nine o'clock news on a Wednesday evening, just before *Sportsnight*, and watched the sad tale of human devastation which habitually passes for the news, and still affirmed in his heart that God is love. What is even more amazing is that he managed to convey this sustaining knowledge of the love of God to ordinary people of his own day, who had every cause to doubt it – the man with an epileptic son, the woman with a dying daughter, the crippled and the blind, the outcast and the leper. So it was that his followers, in the wake of his life and death and resurrection, were able to convince millions of men and women in that ancient and very troubled world that they had good news to bring. Those few inerudite, ill equipped, faulty men managed to outbid the mass media of the ancient world with the convincing message of the love of God and the inward freedom of men. The church of our own day, with its huge, and (contrary to common opinion) still growing membership, is the product of that good news – and is responsible before God for communicating it.

When the presses cease to roll and the newspaper offices are still, when the television screens are blank and the radio is silent; when the world lies in ruins and the scrub grows down to the sea; this news will still be good news – that God has visited his people and that men are saved through Christ for ever.

THE DEMO

Monday, the final day, saw our numbers increase several-fold. We were gaining a new sense of strength. Sections of the Reading Labour movement had joined us.

The column now stretched through country lanes, far out of sight. It took over an hour to pass by. At the midday break we distributed our leaflet. Everyone accepted it and read it.

After a further tiring stretch we reached our objective at last. The final mile was walked in complete silence, along the very edge of the heavily wired perimeter of the Atomic Weapons Research Establishment.

Many must have been surprised by the immensity of the enclosed area and struck by the brutal contrast between the dark, dense forest of rich pine through which we had just marched and the planned waste land of man-made structures with which we were suddenly confronted.

It all had a nightmarish quality. Here was the ultimate reality we had marched against.

Here it was in all its silent horror: those turf-covered mounds of too-geometrical proportions, those metal and concrete pill-boxes of weird but doubtless eminently functional design, those chimneys projecting from ground level, that eerie artificial lake, with its 'No Bathing' signboard and its solitary swan, those unnaturally scattered buildings of utterly incongruous form and size.

Here it lay behind two strong wire trellises, behind a necklace of 'Danger' signs, behind boards soberly stating that police dogs patrolled the perimeter.

Its purpose was the death of men, women and children – and nothing else. It had no redeeming features. It was evil incarnate. It was the final refuge of their class rule, the iron fist inside their velvet glove.

Here it lay, inaccessible, miles from anywhere, mysterious, malevolent, murderous. Here was the sinister factory of death built for the ruling class by their Labour lackeys, built in the last resort for waging war on what was left of the first workers' state in history ...

(D. Widgery, *The Left in Britain 1956–1968*, Peregrine.)

The Aldermaston marches, one of which is described above, had a perfectly humane and sensible objective – to challenge government policy in so far as it saw national security in terms of possession of the nuclear deterrent and a balance of terror. Who indeed could believe that, whatever the short term advantages, long term security could be achieved this way? There is nothing to be said for the proliferation of weapons of destruction and everything to be said for nuclear disarmament. The Aldermaston marches were a great display of idealism on behalf of the young and of the old in pursuit of a rational world order. But one would have to observe, and it is plain from Dr. Widgery's history of the Left, that this idealism was capable of being harnessed for quite different purposes. The great marches in pursuit of peace became the vehicle of those who thought in terms of war – class war indeed but war just the same, every bit as deadly to the body corporate as nuclear weapons.

The same would have to be said about many a demo which has, according to taste, enlivened or disfigured the public life of this nation over the last twenty years. Demos in universities, mounted, one would have to say, with the television cameras in mind, were ostensibly concerned with educational matters but were often organized with quite different objectives in mind, providing as they did confrontation with the forces of

57

law and order. Great rallies in Trafalgar Square were treated to impassioned speeches on matters of genuinely public interest, but were manipulated in such a way as to engage the police in counter-violence. Even a harmless street festival in London for the West Indian population changed either by police intransigence or by race militancy into a serious and potentially dangerous confrontation between the law and a section of the community.

In my study, I have the original of Franklin's cartoon in the Sun newspaper dated September 1, 1976. On the one side is a picture of a metropolitan policeman with a dustbin lid as protection against varying missiles and a little black boy sheltering beside him. It is headed 'White Pigs'. On the other side is a picture of an injured policeman being wheeled along by a black nurse and it is headed 'Black Scum'. It was a telling cartoon showing how easily all truth and compassion can be obscured by the endless repetition of slogans; showing how easy it is to manipulate perfectly legitimate grievances in such a way as to create confrontation and to destroy relationships; illustrating how great forces for social freedom can issue in intolerance and obscurantism.

We need not presume that this is entirely the work of 'conspirators' intent on destroying our society and replacing it with something more in line with their own ambitions – not entirely, although we would be naïve to suppose that they are not present in our midst. Our experience of the demo simply shows how easy it is for a 'demon' to take hold of the most promising enterprises; to overturn the best laid plans, to corrupt high-sounding idealism and leave us infinitely worse off than we were before. Political idealism is not alone in this experience. Religious history has many grisly examples to offer of the same process at work. Our warfare is not always against flesh and blood but against principalities and powers.

If one, however, were to isolate one particular 'demon' secretly at work in contemporary society, it is the demon who is busy discrediting the concept of law. His argument subtly applied to politicians and legislators, to policemen and judges, is as follows. Law, as we experience it on the statute book, is the expression of the convictions and prejudices of the particular society in which we happen to live. So in the west we are still on the whole against murder as a way of life, and heavy penalties attach to that offence. On the other hand we have grown used to adultery, and the destruction of another person's marriage is no longer regarded as culpable. Bearing false witness in a court of law is still an indictable offence, but commercial survival requires that we encourage covetousness. Racial discrimination has become an offence to law as well as to conscience, but it is possible to talk about euthanasia and the disposal of the elderly. Law simply reflects changing habits of mind (so the argument goes) and is devoid of any solemn, binding or universal significance.

But the argument is easily taken a stage further. Law is the product of governmental activity. Successive administrations in this country have prided themselves upon the amount of legislation they have been able to pass through parliament. Too often such legislation is not the result of a consensus but represents the will of the particular party in power. Taken a stage further – and this is by no means a remote possibility – law becomes the means by which the ruling party stays in power and imposes its will upon the whole nation. It becomes an instrument of oppression. We see the end term plainly

59

enough in the constitutional instruments of the USSR, which are motivated by a desire to procure a monolithic state in which religion, or dissent of any kind, is against the law and may therefore be lawfully 'punished'. On the whole, it is perhaps a mark of a reasonable political maturity in the west, that demos (in the cause of freedom) are still permitted. Hyde Park Corner and Trafalgar Square, Grosvenor Place and the Barbican, Aldermaston and Portadown are not just symbols of violence, but assertions of freedom.

Where law simply bows to public opinion or is sustained by an apparatus of secret police, there seems to be only one way forward for those who, for good or bad reasons, dissent from it – and that is to reveal the weakness of the law or the oppressiveness of the law by public demonstration, by the demo. The demo becomes the method by which the law is shown in all its powerlessness, thus reducing its instruments to futility, or in all its oppressiveness, turning policemen into capitalist pigs and judges into political lackeys. Into the social vacuum thus created pour all kinds of operators – those who make their living by violent crime, those who are filled with an irrational rage against society, those who are concerned solely with the achievement of political power, those who see anarchy as a gateway to freedom, those who can only live meaningfully in a state of continuous revolution. Such operators are of course in a minority, but they are highly motivated and powerful; they know how to turn a specious argument and how to win a public hearing. They do not necessarily try to blow up houses of Parliament. They are the demons of the deep, creating an uproar, threatening us with mountainous seas – and hoping to derive a little advantage from it.

The question, therefore, is – can we recover a concept of law which is both permanent and universal, which speaks to the deepest instincts of men and which constitutes a common sentiment around which communities may gather?

In its necessary emphasis upon the free grace of God to the individual believer, the church may well have overlooked its responsibility as a guardian of society and of that law which makes society possible. Hebrew theologians, whatever their extravagances in other respects, never entirely lost hold of this conviction about the role of the people of God, and this conviction finds expression in the literature, the liturgy and the life of the Hebrew people. Perhaps because of the way in which the early books of the Bible have been divided, it is not so evident to us, as it was to them, that the heart of the Old Testament is to be found in the account of the giving of the law at Sinai. Everything before it is preparatory, everything after it is consequential.

The perfect society as represented in Eden is destroyed by man's refusal to obey God's law. The story of Cain and Abel is an illustration of the way in which men forfeit respect for each other and commit murder. The flood follows upon the universal lawlessness of men. The Tower of Babel leads to confusion of tongues and inter-state rivalry. The moral obloquy of Sodom and Gomorrah became a by-word in the ancient world. In short, the book of Genesis purports to describe the origins of our disorders in terms of our lack, or disregard of law.

So the giving of the law at Sinai, with the appropriate visual pomp and acoustic splendour, is the dramatic symbol of God's response to our need; it is an act of loving care; it is a provision for individual and social well-being. And because it is an act of God the giving of that law is seen to be universal, committed indeed to a tiny sector of humanity but intended for all humanity. The decalogue is the gift of God for the healing of the nations, with Israel as its guardian and propagator.

Learned men will, of course, always debate the precise nature of this law – what is original and what is derived; what is temporary and what is eternal; what is merely the product of Israel's particular situation in the world and what is universal. But even to engage in that debate is to accept a psychological position in which it is seen that there is a law of God (however elusive and imprecise) which it is necessary for us to discover and to obey if we are to live at peace with ourselves and each other. The voice at Sinai announced that no man and no society are entitled to create or impose a law after their own hearts, without regard to the law of God. The voice at Sinai announced that law is not an instrument of oppression but a harbinger of freedom. Viewed in that sense, the law is there to protect the weak against the strong, to protect the exploited against the exploiters, to circumscribe the rights of rulers, to establish certain community values, to provide a basis for international understanding and to deliver us as individuals from the tyranny of chance desires.

Thus the law dominates the ancient literature of the Hebrews. The early books of the Bible uncover the need of law and then relate how that law was given to Israel. The prophetic writings bear their testimony to this unchanging law of God and call individuals and nations to obedience to it. The wise men of Israel see in the law the path of wisdom and the secret of happiness. But the law is central also to the worship of Israel. Day after day, year after year, century after century, sacrifice was offered on the sacred mount of Zion in a temple which had at its heart, in the holiest place of all, a small box containing, so it was averred, the tablets of stone which had been received by Moses on Mount Sinai. So the sacred ritual was enacted, the priests performed their sacred acts and the Levites intoned their sacred songs in honour of a God who was represented on earth in the form of law, the ten words which were intended for the blessing of the nations. It is a staggering thought that the series of temples were all built in increasing splendour, in honour of the God of law; that fanatical men lived and died in defence of that law; that far away in Babylon the exiled Hebrew had his windows open towards Jerusalem, from which in the fullness of time, God's law would go forth to the whole earth. This is difficult to believe, but the Hebrews believed it – and if we fall short of that belief, what are we to put in its place, in a world threatened by anarchy?

For the pious Hebrew, the law was not simply the centre of the Hebrew literature, not just the centre of Hebrew worship; it was the centre of his daily life. At every point the law of God, so called, impinged upon his actions. It governed the way he worked and how he took his rest. It governed his relationships with his family and his neighbour. It affected his diet and his hair-style, it was in some ways pain and grief to him – and yet he found in it a way of blessedness. By the time of our Lord, the law had indeed become a heavy yoke, difficult to understand, impossible to observe. It had become a playground for the learned, a bludgeon for the fanatical, a source of pride for the holy and a source of division in the community. But even where the pious Hebrew was defeated by the letter of the law, to his credit he more often than not adhered to the spirit of it. The lifestyle of the Hebrew people was the admiration of the ancient world and many a man of Gentile birth found peace in it.

We do the New Testament a disservice if we allow it to create in our minds certain unnecessary discriminations between the law as the Hebrew understood it and the gospel as the Christian understood it. Even St. Paul, who fell short of none in his strictures of the law as it was understood in his day, still consented to it as 'holy and good'. And as for Jesus of Nazareth, whilst sitting lightly to the minutiae of the law, he spoke in terms of loving devotion to it. He did say that the sabbath was made for man and not man for the sabbath, but he did not dispute that the sabbath was the law of God intended for our blessing. He took the law much further – anger and lust were forbidden, and not just murder and adultery. He saw himself as fulfilling the law, not abrogating it, penetrating to the spirit rather than being bound by the letter, concentrating on the inward attitudes of men not just on their outward actions. In short, he strove to restore the law of God to the people, to extricate it from the grip of the professionals and make it available to mankind. His sermon on the mount in Galilee was a loving, winning, practical recension of that law which Moses had brought down from the mountain in the Sinai wilderness.

The Aldermaston march, the Trafalgar Square rally and the university sit-in seem far removed from the obscure beginnings of law as we discern them through the smoke at Sinai. But the issue at stake is the same. Is law to be an instrument of oppression, an expression of the public will, or an obstacle to freedom; or is it to be regarded as a gift of God to restrain the evil within us, to halt the downward progress to Sodom and

64

Gomorrah, to deliver us from the Babel of international diplomacy? There is many a soul crying out from his moral confusion as the psalmist of old did: 'I am a stranger upon earth; hide not thy commandments from me.'

BIG BROTHER

We owe to George Orwell certain words and expressions which are now part of our verbal currency – *double-think*, *all are equal, but some are more equal than others, four legs good, two legs bad*, and, the most ubiquitous of them all – *Big Brother is watching you*. Here it is then, in context, from that chilling book *Nineteen Eighty-Four*.

It was a bright cold day in April, and the clocks were striking thirteen. Winston Smith, his chin nuzzled into his breast in an effort to escape the vile wind, slipped quickly through the glass doors of Victory Mansions, though not quickly enough to prevent a swirl of gritty dust from entering along with him.

The hallway smelt of boiled cabbage and old rag mats. At one end of it a coloured poster, too large for indoor display, had been tacked to the wall. It depicted simply an enormous face, more than a metre wide: the face of a man of about forty-five, with a heavy black moustache and ruggedly handsome features. Winston made for the stairs. It was no use trying the lift. Even at the best of times it was seldom working, and at present the electric current was cut off during daylight hours. It was part of the economy drive in preparation for Hate Week. The flat was seven flights up, and Winston, who was thirty-nine and had a varicose ulcer above his right ankle, went slowly, resting several times on the way. On each landing, opposite the lift shaft, the poster with the enormous face gazed from the wall. It was one of those pictures which are so contrived that the eyes follow you about when you move. BIG BROTHER IS WATCHING YOU, the caption beneath it ran.

It is always with some surprise that I observe that *Nineteen Eighty-Four* was written as recently as 1949. This, I presume, is because the unfortunate history of Winston Smith has a far distant look, remote from our day, beyond our comprehension. But here we are, with 1984 still ahead, painfully aware that George Orwell's vision is no longer just a vision for half of the inhabitants of the world. In 1949 the enormous face with a heavy black moustache and ruggedly handsome features presided still over the fortunes of the Soviet Union. In 1949 the Chinese People's Republic was formally established and, so the historian writes, 'Mao Tse-tung became the focus of a considerable personality cult.' It was not long before another metre-wide face, without a black moustache but with ruggedly handsome features, was dominating the streets, the shops, the offices, the factories and the apartment buildings of Peking. In 1952 Gamal Abdel Nasser became the leader of a group called the 'Free Officers'. By 1954 General Nasser was Prime Minister, and it was not long before another huge face with ruggedly handsome features was dominating the streets, the shops, the factories, the offices and the apartment buildings of Cairo. In 1959 Dr. Fidel Castro became Prime Minister of Cuba and another face with ruggedly handsome features began to appear on the hoardings in Havana. So, within a decade, Big Brother had extended his rule to well over a thousand million people. How long before the ruggedly handsome features begin to appear on the hoardings in London and New York and Paris?

We are familiar enough with the dynamics of dictatorship – the enfeebled society, the sudden *putsch*, the trappings of democracy and next the naked exercise of power supported by army and police; all followed by imperial adventures – and then the dictator vanishes from the scene as swiftly as he came. The Reich which was to last for a thousand years lasted for precisely fifteen. Such dictatorships are bloodthirsty, destructive, blatantly egotistical – but mercifully brief. The Hebrew people lived out their lives in the ancient world under a succession of tyrants. At times they even tried to emulate them. They wanted a king for themselves who would fight their battles, and ignored Samuel's warning.

'This will be the sort of king who will govern you', he said. 'He will take your sons and make them serve in his chariots and with his cavalry, and will make them run before his chariot. Some he will appoint officers over units of a thousand and units of fifty. Others will plough his fields and reap his harvest; others again will make weapons of war and equipment for mounted troops. He will take your daughters for perfumers, cooks, and confectioners, and will seize the best of your cornfields, vineyards, and olive-yards, and give them to his lackeys. He will take a tenth of your grain and your vintage to give to his eunuchs and lackeys. Your slaves, both men and women, and the best of your cattle and your asses he will seize and put to his own use. He will take a tenth of your flocks, and you yourselves will become his slaves. When that day comes, you will cry out against the king whom you have chosen; but it will be too late, the LORD will not answer you.'

(1 Samuel 8:11–18, New English Bible.)

It is true that the Davidic monarchy had its moments of imperial glory, but they were brief. For the greater part, the Hebrews had to come to terms with an uneasy political existence under the shadow of the Pharaoh, the King of Babylon, a Hellenist monarch, or the Emperor in Rome. It is not surprising that under the pressure of these successive tyrannies, the Hebrews developed a political theology of their own. It is expressed with

68

hindsight in the books of Samuel and vividly illustrated in the book of Daniel.

> At the end of twelve months the king was walking on the roof of the royal palace at Babylon, and he exclaimed, 'Is not this Babylon the great which I have built as a royal residence by my own mighty power and for the honour of my majesty?' The words were still on his lips, when a voice came down from heaven: 'To you, King Nebuchadnezzar, the word is spoken: the kingdom has passed from you. You are banished from the society of men and you shall live with the wild beasts; you shall feed on grass like oxen, and seven times will pass over you until you have learnt that the Most High is sovereign over the kingdom of men and gives it to whom he will.' At that very moment this judgement came upon Nebuchadnezzar. He was banished from the society of men and ate grass like oxen; his body was drenched by the dew of heaven, until his hair grew long like goats' hair and his nails like eagles' talons. (Daniel 4:29–33, New English Bible.)

Tyranny, so the Hebrew theologian is saying, is its own nemesis. It aspires to power and is destroyed by the exercise of it. Yet the author is not so naïve as to imagine that human life on this earth is possible without the exercise of power. Neither does he take refuge in the fond hope that power could be less oppressive if it were distributed along some bureaucratic or democratic model. That only makes it more difficult to locate the centres of power. He simply asserts that power is only safely and legitimately exercised when it is under a greater sovereignty than itself.

> At the end of the appointed time, I, Nebuchadnezzar, raised my eyes to heaven and I returned to my right mind. I blessed the Most High, praising and glorifying the Everliving One:

His sovereignty is never-ending
and his rule endures through all generations;
all dwellers upon earth count for nothing
and he deals as he wishes with the host of heaven;
no one may lay hand upon him
and ask him what he does.

At that very time I returned to my right mind and my majesty and royal splendour were restored to me for the glory of my kingdom. My courtiers and my nobles sought audience of me. I was established in my kingdom and my power was greatly increased. Now I, Nebuchadnezzar, praise and exalt and glorify the King of heaven; for all his acts are right and his ways are just and those whose conduct is arrogant he can bring low.

(Daniel 4:34–37, New English Bible.)

Thus Hebrew theology was more than adequate to the experience of naked tyranny. It could hardly be otherwise; they had learned to live with it through a thousand years and more.

It would be easy to suppose that Big Brother, whose visage we observe on the hoardings of the modern world, is simply an extension of the ancient tyrannies made more oppressive and more durable by the facilities which modern technology supplies. In Winston Smith's room he could not turn off the 'television'; nor was it simply a means of viewing – it was a means of being viewed. Big Brother was always watching him. So the modern instruments of propaganda and surveillance can effectively entrench the ruling party, thus ensuring a kind of immunity to the democratic uprising, the sudden *putsch*, even the armed intervention from outside. What is more, this physical control of the population can be sustained by an increasing mental and cultural control which, as in George Orwell's book, can produce a language in which the age-long concepts of truth and justice can no longer be expressed and in which familiar terms can be used to express precisely the opposite of their original meaning.

The Ministry of Truth – Minitrue, in Newspeak – was startlingly different from any other object in sight. It was an enormous pyramidal structure of glittering white concrete, soaring up, terrace after terrace, 300 metres into the air. From where Winston stood it was just possible to read, picked out on its white face in elegant lettering, the three slogans of the Party:

WAR IS PEACE

FREEDOM IS SLAVERY

IGNORANCE IS STRENGTH

So we could say that Big Brother is simply the Pharaoh, the great king, the Caesar of the ancient world writ large. The image and superscription on the coin has become the huge face on the wall.

Yet there is one important difference. The tyrants of the ancient world often took to themselves divine prerogatives – and indeed required emperor worship from their subjects. But it was obvious to most of their subjects that a tyrant fell far short of divinity. It is difficult to take seriously a god who makes his horse a consul, so the Greek dramatist engaged in a certain friendly ribaldry at the expense of the god-monarch. On the whole, therefore, outside the immediate court, the ancient rulers were taken for what they were – adventurers who had had a bit of luck, power-hungry men who revelled in their power, gods with feet of clay. So the book of Daniel describes one such tyrant.

This image, huge and dazzling, towered before you, fearful to behold. The head of the image was of fine gold, its breast and arms of silver, its belly and thighs of bronze, its legs of iron, its feet part iron and part clay. While you looked, a stone was hewn from a mountain, not by human hands; it struck the image on its feet of iron and clay and shattered them. Then the iron, the clay, the bronze, the silver, and the gold, were all shattered to fragments and were swept away like chaff before the wind from a threshing-floor in summer, until no trace of them remained.

(Daniel 2:31–35, New English Bible.)

What is distinctive about the Big Brother of the modern world is that he makes no claim to divinity, requires no worship and is not even part of a pantheon. Yet by subtle propaganda he, or those around him, create an image which is all the more powerful for its ability to suggest the lineaments of the eternal god. His face dominates the market place where once the Holy Rood stood. He is not only omnipotent (that we can learn to live with); he is kind. It is not only a hand-some face that dominates the market-place; it is wise and far-seeing and passionate. Behold thy god. What are we to say to such a person? How do we resist him? Here is no evil man inviting the wrath of a subject populace, provoking rebellion, stamping out dissent; but one who deserves thanks for his unspeakable generosity, praise for his unsearchable wisdom, love for his costly sacrifice on our behalf.

We are in the presence of a singularly dangerous phenomenon and we may well ask whether our theology is adequate for it. The answer is likely to be no, because theology invariably springs out of the life experience of a people and we have little life experience of Big Brother. It is no longer quite enough to say that human tyrants rule only by divine permission and that in the end they will be blown away like the chaff. That is bound to be

72

as true of Big Brother today as it was of the tyrants of yesterday, but it is small comfort for those who find themselves not simply in physical but in intellectual and spiritual subjection to the Big Brother who is watching them every day, reading their thoughts, weighing their attitudes, judging their aspirations. It may, however, be some comfort to those thousand million who have to live with Big Brother and the other thousand million who may well have to learn to live with him, if we attempt first of all to account for this phenomenon and then to interpret it.

It is not difficult to account for if your mind is in any way attuned to the abiding needs of the human psyche. Atheism is impossible. If, so the theologians of the Bible assert, you deny the existence of the true God, you invariably make a home for a false one. We cannot live in a world from which God is banished. So the rationalism of the nineteenth century, for all its great and necessary contributions to human society, is the womb from which Big Brother comes. The fact is that Big Brother does not even have to assert his authority; he does not even have to call for worship. He is worshipped because there is no one else to worship. God is dead; long live the gods. Big Brother is the product of necessity and we shall have to live with him until we recapture a conviction about the 'kingdom of God'. Kingdom of God theology, as we might call it, is the product of the Hebrew experience of human tyranny. It reflects the ever present but often unexpressed dependence of the human mind upon a reality which is greater than the transitory realities by which we are surrounded. So Jeremiah puts it, to a people marvellously endowed with a sense of the living God and yet who exchanged their God for a lie.

These are the words of the Lord:
What fault did your forefathers find in me,
that they wandered far from me,
pursuing empty phantoms and themselves becoming empty;
that they did not ask, 'Where is the LORD,
who brought us up from Egypt,
and led us through the wilderness,
through a country of deserts and shifting sands,
a country barren and ill-omened, where no man ever trod,
no man made his home?'
I brought you into a fruitful land
to enjoy its fruit and the goodness of it;
but when you entered upon it you defiled it
and made the home I gave you loathsome.
The priests no longer asked, 'Where is the LORD?'
Those who handled the law had no thought of me,
the shepherds of the people rebelled against me;
the prophets prophesied in the name of Baal
and followed gods powerless to help.
Therefore, I will bring a charge against you once more,
says the LORD,
against you and against your descendants.
Cross to the coasts and islands of Kittim and see,
send to Kedar and consider well,
see whether there has been anything like this:
has a nation ever changed its gods,
although they were no gods?
But my people have exchanged their Glory
for a god altogether powerless.
Stand aghast at this, you heavens,
tremble in utter despair,
says the LORD.
Two sins have my people committed:
they have forsaken me,
a spring of living water,
and they have hewn out for themselves cisterns,
cracked cisterns that can hold no water.
(Jeremiah 2:5–13, New English Bible.)

Big Brother now dominates the market place, where once the Holy Rood stood; it is one thing to account for it, quite another thing to interpret it. Is the figure of Big Brother substantially different from the figure that looks down upon us from the Holy Rood and from a million stained-glass windows and from the art galleries of Europe?

There is a sense in which the figure who emerges for us out of the pages of the New Testament is the biggest Big Brother of all. He appears to arrogate to himself divine qualities. He is omnipotent over the waves of the sea, over the ravages of disease, over the demon. And he is kind above all other.

Yet there are features which at first sight contradict that picture. He sets his face against propaganda. He tells the beneficiaries of his omnipotent love that they are to tell no one about it. He resists the desire of his disciples to make him into a cult figure. He regards desire to impress the multitudes and to achieve social miracles as a temptation of the devil. He rebuked Peter for wishing to cast him in the role of the biggest Big Brother of all: 'Get behind me Satan. Yours are the thoughts of man, not the thoughts of God.' But perhaps the most astonishing utterance of all is the one attributed to him by Mark and followed in this respect by Luke: 'Why do you call me good? None is good save one, even God.' This was altogether too much for Matthew, or at least for those responsible for some editions of Matthew's gospel, where the phrase is changed to 'Why do you ask me concerning that which is good?' But in biblical interpretation the golden rule is always to accept the more difficult reading; and in the eyes of the early Christians Mark's is a very hard reading indeed. But there it stands, embedded in the text, representing if there ever was one an original saying of the Christ.

Even more striking, however, is the fact that the Christian church was able to tolerate an even harder saying – the visible word that is to be read in the experience of Calvary. This is no Big Brother looking down from a hoarding with ruggedly handsome features, but a man haggard and broken, despairing and defeated, with no beauty that we should desire him, like a root out of dry ground without form or comeliness, despised and rejected by men, a man of sorrows and acquainted with grief. This is not the kind of Big Brother we want – serene and confident, omnipotent and kind. And yet for two thousand years the Rood has dominated the market place – and will dominate it again – leaving only as a distant memory in some far-away world a face with ruggedly handsome features which aspired briefly to the domination of mankind.

There are a thousand million who, in varying degrees, are subject to Big Brother. There are another thousand million who are subject with varying degrees of conviction to the Christ – not for their comfort necessarily, but for their freedom; not for their security but for their joy; not as a magic talisman but as an unfailing resource. The book of Revelation speaks thus of one Big Brother – 'The whole world went after the beast in wondering admiration.' But only for a time.

THE GURU

On the London underground, with an advertisement for women's stockings on his right and an invitation to holiday in Tenerife on his left, with a notice of a sleazy film above and fervent claims for a man's deodorant below, is the picture of the guru. Here indeed is no metre-wide face, no ruggedly handsome features. He is a very little brother and he is not looking at you. He sits there in traditional posture seemingly indifferent to the multitudes which pour up and down on the escalator, inviting you to an experience of transcendental meditation in Kensington or Maida Vale or Kilburn. This little brother is not looking at you nor necessarily even at God. He is, in the words of Father Dechanet in his book *Christian Yoga* (Search Press),

> looking for nothing other than himself, his true self, from the knowledge of which he is debarred by a whole world of illusion. He is a challenge to the world, spun about in the whirl of business, enslaved to countless technical inventions, severed from God and from the world of the spirit.

And so it is that a man here and a woman there – carried along in the turgid stream of mankind, to the office and the factory – up or down the escalator gazes upon that face and wonders whether the secret of life might not be found in an obscure room in Maida Vale or Kensington or Kilburn. For there is no doubt that the old nineteenth-century faith which we call secular humanism has utterly collapsed.

We of the late twentieth century have inherited an

impoverished, broken-down estate. We live surrounded by the signs of certain past grandeur – the decaying gardens, the tottering walls, the overgrown drive – but we are helpless to restore it. The bitter events of the twentieth century, including two world wars, the nuclear bomb, mounting pollution and widespread social malaise, have destroyed for ever the vision of a world made fit by technological advance for heroes to live in. But, of course, we labour phrenetically to keep the fabric up, to maintain the state of life which our ancestors have left us with, to make the wretched thing pay, whilst in our hearts we know that the past is past and we are enslaved to a lost cause. It is not surprising, therefore, that the guru wins many disciples amongst the young and the sensitive and the dissatisfied. They can no longer find fulfilment in the kind of lives they are invited to live, so perfectly characterized in this charming verse by Kenneth Fearing:

> And wow he died as wow he lived,
> Going whop to the office, and blooie
> home to sleep and
> biff got married and bam had children
> and oof got fired.
> Zowie did he live and zowie did he die.
> (Quoted by Stanley Jones, *Abundant Living*, Hodder & Stoughton.)

If the guru is a challenge to the world and to those residual values which some of us still hold dear, he is a challenge also to the church in its almost total failure to respond to this deeply felt need of the human heart. What have we been doing, I wonder, that men should have to turn to the guru? The apparatus of the eternal is everywhere around us in the church. We have had our own outstanding gurus, ornaments of the church in their generation. We have our ancient buildings, still challenging in the name of God the crude structures by which they are surrounded in many a great conurbation. We have a day set apart every week for the contemplation of the eternal and the real. In the Church of England alone we have twelve thousand parochial clergymen entirely committed to the initiating of our people into the mysteries of life. We have an unfailing source of knowledge in the Bible, an unfailing source of life in the sacraments. Potentially, at every point, we challenge the temporal in the name of the eternal. And yet men have to go to Kensington and Maida Vale and Kilburn.

I never travel on the London underground on what I am pleased to think is necessary business on behalf of the church without being rebuked by that little brother sitting there – so often offering stones for bread, scorpions for fish; and everywhere the hungry sheep look up and are not fed. Here am I 'going whop to the office' followed by the unseeing eyes of the guru. And so it is that millions upon millions in the western world see in the church only what we sometimes call, in a hateful phrase, 'organized religion' – outworn moral attitudes, irrelevant public gestures and, most damning of all, formal worship.

Christians who read this book will know that it is not as bad as that, but that is how it seems. The great unchurched would no more turn to the church for spiritual illumination and an experience of reality than they would go to the barber to have their teeth out. But on my bookshelves, behind my head as I write, I have Thomas Merton on *The Silent Life*; Carlo Carretto on *Letters from the Desert*; F. C. Happold on *The Journey Inwards*; Henri Nouwen on *Reaching Out*; Morton Kelsy on *Encounter with God*; Anthony Bloom on *Living Prayer*; Olive Wyon on *The Desire for God*; Rollo May on *Man's*

Search for Himself and Father Dechanet on *Christian Yoga*. We are rich in spiritual resources; we have a never failing barrel of meal, an all-sufficient cruse of oil; thousands in the wilderness looking for sustenance and we with our five loaves and two small fishes adequate for every need. In every parish of the land we have a guru.

In so far as the guru stands within the great sacred yoga tradition, which many of them do, he proposes to himself the following:

> ... purity – outward cleanliness, and purity of heart; contentedness – non-attachment to things and events, manifesting itself in calm, joy, a special kind of happiness, and the absence of reaction to what might be called the pinpricks of life; austerity of living – never going beyond the limits set by discretion in thought, word or deed; self-knowledge – the gradual understanding of one's being and of one's self; and lastly, becoming attached to the divine, and yielding up one's being entirely to a personal God.
> (Dechanet, *Christian Yoga*.)

Father Dechanet concedes that the practice of yoga is linked with philosophical and religious beliefs absolutely incompatible with Christian dogma, but not that it is necessarily dependent on them. So it could be that the guru is offering us a technique

> that allows man – when this is fitting – to establish himself in silence; not merely away from noise, but effectively in the silence of the senses, desires and human passions, in the silence of mind, banishing preoccupying thoughts and worries, accepting above all to remain silent so that the Holy Spirit of God may now and then make its voice heard, and the spirit of the man be listening.

But we have to go further and ask what is the biblical and theological basis on which we may go beyond the 'technique' and discover the living God in all his fullness; the God of Abraham, Isaac and Jacob, the God and father of our Lord Jesus Christ.

To experience the spirituality of the Bible is to experience something distinctly but mysteriously different from the spirituality we associate with the guru in particular and Indian religion in general. The outward phenomena associated with both may appear very much the same – the great feats of the ascetic, the flight from the world into the wilderness, the long hours of prayer, the ecstasy, the miracles, intolerance with the tolerance of men. Elijah, Ezekiel, John the Baptist and those like them who despised the world are spiritual athletes not so different in appearance from their counterparts across the Indian Ocean. But it is in fact more than the Indian Ocean which divides them. Their view of reality is different, their objectives are at variance with each other.

This may best be illustrated from what the reader may find a somewhat tiresome excursus on vocabulary. It is a mark of the spiritual poverty of the western world, and of its ancestor the Greek world, that the Greek, and for that matter the English language have virtually only one word for prayer – which can mean almost anything in the minds of those who use that word or in any sense allow their lives to be affected by it. It is strictly a religious word and is hardly ever used outside religious parlance.

The Hebrew language, on the other hand, has at least fourteen words which purport to describe man's relationship with the ineffable and the divine. The striking fact is that these words are not exclusively religious; they may be found in ordinary secular affairs; they may apply to a man's relationship to his employer as well as his relationship to God. The nature of this vocabulary is instructive. It suggests that there is no hard and fast distinction to be made between sacred and secular, between temporal and eternal, between spiritual and physical. In the main, these words may be divided etymologically between those which, as it were, act upon God and those which wait for God to act. They describe on the one hand a dynamic relationship by which, as Luther said, we bring it about that God hastens, when otherwise he would not so hasten, and on the other an attitude of waiting, tension, silence, faith, hope. 'Waiting, not seeking, we go our way,' as Buber put it (Martin Buber, *I And Thou*, T. & T. Clark).

It is at this level that we must make the most striking distinction between the Hebrew prophet and the Indian guru. The guru thinks in terms of abstraction from the world, of passivity in the face of existence, of contempt for the activities of men, and of the ultimate vision. There is a sense in which the Hebrew prophet begins where the guru leaves off. He invariably begins with vision he has not sought or desired, for which he has made little spiritual preparation and which is totally unexpected. It is a vision of the living God sending him into the world of men. So Isaiah's vision of God in the temple is not given as a reward for lengthy spiritual endurance, nor as an invitation to a life of abstraction. The vision is immediately followed by the command to the service of God in the world – and Isaiah's life thereafter was one of intense preoccupation with the lives of men and the affairs of nations.

The same could be said, in varying degrees, of every prophet, and John the Baptist (the last of them) was true to his pedigree when he came out of the wilderness and engaged in the squalid affairs of an oriental-style monarchy – having things to say about brutal interrogations by soldiers; about sharing goods with other people; about being content with your wages. The prophet is invariably concerned with the kingdom of God on earth; he does not wait for heaven or Nirvana. He does not prescribe exercises, but summons to obedience to the Word of God revealed, the Voice of God heard. So Father Dechanet –

> The Christian in praying does not have to search for his own self nor to forget himself in the manner of Orientals, but to open himself to the word of God, for it is solely in this and by this that he can find himself and exist.

The word *guru* means simply 'teacher'. The equivalent Semitic word is applied invariably to Jesus of Nazareth. He too appears to have prescribed no exercises; he sets his face deliberately, as it seems, against asceticism and he is, to the disgust of the religious of his day, too fond of parties. So far is he removed from the traditional picture of the religious teacher that his disciples have to insist that he teaches them to pray. His prayer is no series of *mantras* but a simple prayer, in the prophetic style, asking that God's kingdom may come and his will may be done on earth. He does not rest on some esoteric tradition, suitable only for initiates. Rather he expresses in his own person and in his own activity the open Word of God available to all, capable of being heard, capable of being obeyed.

The word meaning 'to teach' in the Hebrew language invariably means, as far as I am able to judge, to teach the law, not to spin a web of secret knowledge. Jesus' view of life is that God has exhibited his will in the law and the prophets and that it is in conformity with that will that true blessedness is to be found. Like the guru

83

he gathers to himself a select group of disciples, but unlike the guru he makes them prophets and evangelists, apostles and organizers. They stand before kings; they argue with the learned; they make regulations; they disagree with each other – and they die the death which their involvement in the world makes inevitable.

We must thank God for the guru – he is a challenge to the world and a rebuke to the church, but the God he worships is not the God of Abraham, Isaac or Jacob nor the God and father of our Lord Jesus Christ. But as he sits there, with the advertisements for women's stockings on his left and an invitation to holiday in Tenerife on his right, with a notice of a sleazy film above and a man's deodorant beneath, I welcome him to the London underground.

POLLUTION

The medium, as Marshall McLuhan said and the professionals have been saying ever since, is the message. Television is an entertainment medium. Whatever the intention of a producer, whether he has education or information or insight into current affairs, he fails as an agent of the mass medium unless at the same time he also entertains. In that sense the professionals are right – the medium is the message.

For many months the famous BBC programme *Doomwatch* dominated our screens one evening a week. It was a well-conceived, well-researched programme, enjoying the services of three distinguished actors. The senior scientist in the programme and his two junior assistants constituted a department of government called 'Doomwatch'. They were required, on varying occasions, to deal with a nuclear device, genetic engineering, an outbreak of plague, the malfunctioning of a chemical plant and many another threat to human existence here on earth. Would it be too much to say that I enjoyed the programmes – at a safe distance from the nuclear device, the plague and the malfunctioning chemical plant? The programmes, whatever else they may have been, constituted part of the entertainment industry. We grew accustomed to the harassed face of the senior scientist, to the outbursts and the self-questionings of his assistants and to the whole panorama of technical expertise used for dubious ends.

But then there was the case of the malfunctioning of a

chemical plant in Italy – which was for real; men, women and children pay the cost for that malfunctioning in the loss of health and the desolation of their lands. Then there was the case of a pesticide in Michigan which, by an unfortunate accident, was inadequately labelled and was fed to the animals. We have yet to discover the final effects of that little accident. Meanwhile, many a mother walks in fear for the future of her children. So *Doomwatch* was not so far-fetched as we thought at the time. Doom is nearer than we might have supposed; it lurks hidden within many an innocent looking chemical plant, in a row of test tubes in a laboratory, in an unidentified package in a dockside warehouse.

The dramatic failure of a chemical plant and its consequences for the countryside around are there for everyone to see on the nine o'clock news. The inadequate labelling of a sack makes the headlines for a day or two – though, alas, is quickly forgotten except by those who suffer from the results. But the growth of the economy and, to be fair, even the needs of the third world require from us more and more elaborate technical processes which achieve immediate and necessary results, without much regard for the long-term consequences for the ecology of the earth. It is hardly possible to make a dramatic and entertaining programme of these slow, hidden, destructive processes which are at work in the streams, the hedgerows, the soil and the atmosphere. It is of this more insidious process that the Ehrlichs write in their book *Population, Resources, Environment*:

> The global polluting and exploiting activities of the developed countries are even more serious than their internal problems. Spaceship Earth is now filled to capacity or beyond and is running out of food. And yet the people

travelling first class are, without thinking, demolishing the ship's already overstrained life-support systems. The food-producing mechanism is being sabotaged. The devices that maintain the atmosphere are being turned off. The temperature-control system is being altered at random. Thermonuclear bombs, poison gases, and super-germs have been manufactured and stockpiled by people in the few first-class compartments for possible future use against other first-class passengers in their competitive struggles for dwindling resources – or perhaps even against the expectant but weaker masses of humanity in steerage. But, unaware that there is no one at the controls of their ship, many of the passengers ignore the chaos or view it with cheerful optimism, convinced that everything will turn out all right.

The plain fact of the matter is that we are tampering with processes we do not understand, ensuring for ourselves a standard of living at the cost of future generations; we are polluting the earth.

It is not to be supposed that pollution is a wholly novel experience for mankind. But it was not in the main self-generated. Listen to this, for example, from the book of the prophet Joel written in about the fourth century BC:

A fire devoureth before them; and behind them a flame burneth: the land is as the garden of Eden before them, and behind them a desolate wilderness; yea, and nothing shall escape them. The appearance of them is as the appearance of horses; and as horsemen, so shall they run. Like the noise of chariots on the tops of mountains shall they leap, like the noise of a flame of fire that devoureth the stubble, as a strong people set in battle array. Before their face the people shall be much pained: all faces shall gather blackness. They shall run like mighty men; they shall climb the wall like men of war; and they shall march every one

87

on his ways, and they shall not break their ranks: Neither shall one thrust another; they shall walk every one in his path: and when they fall upon the sword, they shall not be wounded. They shall run to and fro in the city; they shall run upon the wall, they shall climb up upon the houses; they shall enter in at the windows like a thief. The earth shall quake before them; the heavens shall tremble: the sun and the moon shall be dark, and the stars shall withdraw their shining.

(Joel 2:3–10, Authorized Version.)

So is described the most terrible of the scourges of the Bible lands – the swarm of locusts. Here is a modern description:

They fill the air, darkening the sky, the noise of their wings resembles the pattering of the heavy rain, they fly with great rapidity and towards nightfall they alight wherever they may happen to be and such are their numbers that they often break the branches of the trees to which they cling ... the black larvae now spread like a pall over the land, eating every green thing, even stripping the bark of the trees ... they choke the wells and streams which are often filled by their innumerable carcases and so defiled, their waters are no longer drinkable.

(G. E. Post, *Hastings Dictionary of the Bible*, T. & T. Clark.)

The locusts have plagued the earth for thousands of years and we perhaps too easily assume that we now have them under control. But that is not the view of the *New Scientist* in its issue of March 17, 1977. Tony Loftas in his article, though hopeful of the future, says this:

A plague of locusts is long overdue. The last major outbreak of this age-old pestilence was in 1968, but this was a mere shadow of earlier incidents: from 1949 to 1963 the plagues raged back and forth virtually unchecked.

It is difficult for us in the west to imagine what this age-old pestilence meant to those who suffered from it – not a leaf on the tree, not a blade of grass, the vineyards stripped and all hopes of a harvest lost. So the prophet Joel could say of them that 'the land is as the garden of Eden before them and behind them a desolate wilderness.' I find myself wondering whether such future generations as survive will not look back upon our own self-generated pollution and say the same of us – before them the land was as the garden of Eden and after them a desolate wilderness.

Accustomed as they were to plague and pestilence, to sudden death and slow starvation, the Hebrews did not reserve their ultimate horror for the physical pollution of the earth, but for its moral pollution. The word *pollution* is a familiar one in the English versions of the Bible. The Hebrews could speak of the land being polluted with idols, polluted with disobedience to the law, polluted with injustice and exploitation. The prophets were loud in their denunciation of their fellow countrymen for thus polluting the moral and spiritual atmosphere of the world. To them the iniquities of the home, the street and the synagogue, the market and the council chamber, were infinitely more destructive of the 'ecology' than even the dreaded swarm of locusts or the plague that strikes at night.

It is strange that the so-called liberal civilization of the western world is preoccupied, almost to a fault, with the dangers to the physical environment; yet is oddly indifferent, except at certain chosen points, to the pollution of the spiritual environment. Thus it is considered dangerous to allow a typhoid contact to work in a restaurant kitchen or a cholera suspect to walk in the streets, whilst some of the other deadly activities of the human race are permitted relative freedom – the sadist film and the sex shop. We are heavily, not to say oppressively protected in the interests of physical health; we are at liberty to destroy ourselves and each other in the interests of freedom and self-satisfaction. There are many well-heeled operators in the streets and clubs of our cities, who, like the locusts of a past age, find a garden of Eden ahead of them and leave behind a desolate wilderness. They are at ease, but they choke the well-springs of life, destroying the green shoots and polluting the earth.

It is sometimes said that the prophets of Israel were Pelagians, that is to say that they suffered from the peculiarly English illusion that you have only to identify the evil to denounce it, to exercise good-will and watch it being solved. It is true that they addressed themselves to the problems of their day with the conviction that those whom they addressed were free to respond to their call, free to amend their ways, free to recover a healthy relationship with God and with their fellows. It was perhaps inevitably left to others in the Hebrew tradition to uncover the depths of the human heart and to show that we were not free to repent and to amend. It is in this tradition that we find the 'evil inclination' of which the Rabbis spoke. It lies at the root of the famous story of Adam and Eve, who did indeed find a garden of Eden to live in and left it a desolate wilderness.

So the word *pollution* came to apply not simply to the physical pollution of the earth nor even its moral and spiritual pollution, but to that inner state of pollution which is the experience of every Adam and Eve. So the author of the book of Job – 'How can man be just with God or how can he be clean that is born of a woman?' Hear too the cry of the Psalmist:

> Behold, I was shapen in wickedness: and in sin hath my
> mother conceived me. But lo, thou requirest truth in the
> inward parts: and shalt make me to understand wisdom
> secretly. Thou shalt purge me with hyssop, and I shall be
> clean: thou shalt wash me, and I shall be whiter than
> snow. Thou shalt make me hear of joy and gladness: that
> the bones which thou hast broken may rejoice. Turn thy
> face from my sins: and put out all my misdeeds.
>
> (Psalm 51:5–9, *Book of Common Prayer*.)

This sense of inner pollution, expressed thus in literary
form, had its counterpart in the liturgical services of the
Jewish year. The Day of Atonement, for the sins of the
people, had as its objective the ritual removal of that
inner uncleanness, the awareness of which was so distinctive of Hebrew religion as a whole. Other nations
had their law codes; other nations recognized their
faults; other nations had days of repentance. But no
other nation was able so poignantly to give expression
to that universal sense of inner pollution. Universal, you
may ask? Does it not rather reflect an unhealthy preoccupation with sin, from which we have now been
liberated? I refer you then to a contemporary experience
of inner pollution:

> This morning at the library, when the Autodidact came
> to say good-morning to me, it took me ten seconds to
> recognize him. I saw an unknown face which was barely a
> face. And then there was his hand, like a fat maggot in my
> hand. I let go of it straight away and the arm fell back
> limply ...
>
> Objects ought not to touch, since they are not alive. You
> use them, you put them back in place, you live among
> them: they are useful, nothing more. But they touch me, it's
> unbearable. I am afraid of entering in contact with them,
> just as if they were living animals.

Now I see; I remember better what I felt the other
day on the sea-shore when I was holding that pebble. It
was a sort of sweet disgust. How unpleasant it was! And it
came from the pebble, I'm sure of that, it passed from the
pebble into my hands. Yes, that's it, that's exactly it: a sort
of nausea in the hands.

(Sartre, *Nausea*, Penguin.)

The only difference between Jean-Paul Sartre and the
theologians and liturgists of Israel is that he experienced
nausea as part of the very nature of the world, not
simply as a feature of the human condition. He had a
vivid sense of the desolate wilderness but little of the
garden of Eden. Or listen to Albert Camus, another
twentieth-century writer, as he describes the human
condition at the end of his novel *The Plague*:

And, indeed, as he listened to the cries of joy rising from
the town, Rieux remembered that such joy is always
imperilled. He knew what those jubilant crowds did not
know but could have learned from books: that the plague
bacillus never dies or disappears for good; that it can lie
dormant for years and years in furniture and linen-chests;
that it bides its time in bedrooms, cellars, trunks, and bookshelves; and that perhaps the day would come when, for the
bane and the enlightening of men, it roused up its rats
again and sent them forth to die in a happy city.

(Camus, *The Plague*, Penguin.)

The sense of inner pollution, therefore, may not be a
universal experience (most of us live too near the surface
for that) but it is an inexpugnable element in the psy-
chology of the race, ancient Jewish or modern French.

The Hebrews were well aware of the problem and
braver than most in exposing it. They struggled with it
in literature and ritual. Yet they manifestly failed to
provide any solution to it. The lambs indeed were slain

on the holy hill of Zion, the high priest entered the holy place once a year for the sins of the people, but the people found no ease of heart, no permanent deliverance. Even the greatest of their sons, perceptive and zealous though they were, found no solace. Too often, as they knew, they found a garden of Eden ahead of them and left behind them a desolate wilderness. I perceive, as St. Paul said in surely one of the most poignant descriptions of the human condition, that 'nothing good dwells within me, that is in my flesh; I can will what is right but I cannot do it. For I do not do the good I want but the evil I do not want is what I do.'

It is at this point that Christian faith reaches far out beyond the point to which its predecessors had even aspired. John the Baptist was the first to perceive that in Jesus he beheld 'the Lamb of God that takes away the sin of the world'. It was presumably this conviction which laid so heavily on our Lord's heart as he drew near to the final dreadful denouement in Jerusalem. The lambs had been slain in pursuit of the ancient quest for cleanness of heart. The Lamb of God was now to be slain as an offering for sin, once for all. It is all the more striking, therefore, that that strange, still inexplicable section of the book of Isaiah, which we call the fourth servant song, should contain the word which is elsewhere used in the Old Testament for 'pollution'. A normal translation reads as follows:

> But he was wounded for our transgressions, he was bruised for our iniquities: the chastisement of our peace was upon him; and with his stripes we are healed.
> (Isaiah 53:5, Authorized Version.)

The verb is in a relatively unusual form but it certainly would be legitimate to translate it: 'He was polluted for

93

our transgressions.' It is perhaps immaterial precisely what the ancient prophet had in mind, but the general sense remains – in some mysterious way the Lamb of God associated himself with the deepest degradations of the human spirit, and took them away. Unlike the rest of us, our Lord finds a desolate wilderness ahead and leaves behind him a garden of Eden.

THE CONURBATION

It has often been remarked that the Bible begins with a garden and ends with a city. This is true in the narrow literary sense that the story of the garden of Eden comes at the beginning of the book of Genesis and the vision of the New Jerusalem at the end of the book of Revelation. Whether we may infer from that literary 'accident' that the true progress of mankind is from simple agricultural tribal structure to the great conurbations of the modern world, is another matter. Perhaps I may burden the reader with a few reflections on the theological process at work in the Bible as distinct from the accident by which the books reached their present places in the sacred canon.

The book of Genesis attends to the deepest problems of human society by means of an historical retrospect, but it is itself a mature theological book arising out of a sophisticated theological tradition. There is a sense in which the author is more concerned with the future than with the past, regarding the garden of Eden as something yet to be achieved, not simply lost in an immemorial past. The time will come, perhaps he is saying, when men and women may live together in ordered relationships with each other, doing the will of God and cultivating his gifts in obedience to his will. To put it more technically, the author is more concerned with eschatology than with ancient history.

As for the city in the book of Revelation, it is a city which comes down from heaven and it is not necessarily the product of a long and painful historical process. Perhaps, indeed, the author wishes us to understand that the great cities of his own time fall so far short of the will of God that only a mighty act of God himself can produce the city of men's dreams. But we are handling literary material here of great subtlety and he would be a bold man who would dogmatize upon the implications of the simple fact that mankind begins in a garden and ends in a city.

For a moment then we suspend decision whilst we look at that singular product of modern times – the great conurbation.

But have we the right to single out the great conurbation as one of the signs of the times? In Alexandria, we are told, founded three hundred years before Christ, there were three hundred thousand freedmen – which suggests a total population of at least twice that size. Opinions vary about the size of Nineveh which figures in the book of Jonah. It was the administrative capital of Sennacherib seven centuries before Christ, and it may well have had well over half a million inhabitants. Thebes, the capital of ancient Egypt, dating from nearly 2,000 BC, may well have been a city of much the same size. Barbara Ward tells us in her book *The Home of Man* that Ch'ang-an, the Tang Capital, was a city of two million people in our Dark Ages.

So the inclusion of the conurbation amongst the signs of our time may be no more than yet another illustration of the chronological insularity which is so typical of the twentieth century. Not all our problems are modern problems. Town planning, suburban development, inner-city decline, the urban proletariat are as much the problem of ancient Thebes as they are of modern Birmingham. Does not the city remain in essence what it has always been – a dangerous but fascinating expression of the skills, culture, squalors and sins of mankind?

... its smells too, and above all its colourful, polyglot inhabitants, caught in one vivid phrase after another, glimpsed for a moment and then gone – the African poling his felucca up the Tiber, with a cargo of cheap rancid oil; the plump smooth successful lawyer riding above the heads of the crowd in his litter; the homosexual fluttering his eyelids as he applies his make-up, or wearing a chiffon gown, near-transparent, to plead a case in court; the ageing gladiator, straight out of Hogarth or Rowlandson, 'helmet-scarred, a great wen on his nose, an unpleasant discharge from one constantly weeping eye'; a lady of quality, her large thighs wrapped in coarse puttees, panting and blowing at sword-drill; the downtrodden teacher and his resentful pupils, conning lamp-blackened texts of Virgil before daybreak; the sadistic mistress who sits reading the daily gazette or examining dress-material while one of her slaves is being flogged in the same room; the would-be poet giving a recital in a cheap, peeling hired hall, with his claque of freedmen distributed at strategic points through the audience; the fat, horsy consul Lateranus, swearing stable oaths, untrussing his own hay, or boozing with matelots and escaped convicts in some dockside tavern; the contemptible trimmers hurrying down to boot Sejanus's corpse in the ribs ('and make sure our slaves watch us') while sneering at the rabble for its opportunism; the miser hoarding fish-scraps in September; the squad of slaves with fire-buckets guarding a millionaire's objets d'art; the court-material presided over by a group of hobnailed old colour-sergeants; the temple-robber scraping gold leaf from the statues of unprotesting deities; the sizzle of sacrificial offerings, the roar of the crowd at the races, beggars blowing kisses, the carver flourishing his knives, fortune-tellers, whores, confidence-men, politicians – it is an endless and kaleidoscopic panorama.

So might be described any city, ancient or modern. This happens to be a description of ancient Rome from Peter Green's introduction to the *Satires* of Juvenal in Penguin Books. For Rome read London or Paris or New York or Tokyo. There is, as the ancient wisdom writer said, nothing, absolutely nothing new under the sun:

This view might seem to be sustained by the general argument of Professor Galbraith's book *The Age of Uncertainty*. The city begins as a political household:

> Over the centuries nothing has been so thought to enhance royal personality, competence in armed slaughter apart, as the architectural embellishment of the seat of government. Rome, Persepolis, Angkor, Constantinople, Paris, Versailles, the Forbidden City, Leningrad née St. Petersburg, Vienna, Segovia and literally a hundred other wonders are the result.

(Galbraith, *Age of Uncertainty*, BBC Publications.)

Then comes the so-called merchant city, dominated by the guild hall and the town hall, to which were added occasionally the cathedral and the church. Then comes the industrial city artificially created by the early industrialists as a location for their mills and a habitation for their workers. And then finally, in Professor Galbraith's analysis, the metropolis – London, New York, Tokyo. Professor Galbraith avoids the use of the term *conurbation*, as well he might, for it is an ugly, imprecise word; the Oxford Etymological Dictionary calls it somewhat bleakly 'an urban aggregate'.

An urban aggregate which seems to exist not as a political household, or as a mercantile centre, or as an industrial city, but just as itself. It is there – sprawling over the scene, intersected by countless streets, swamping the individuality of ancient villages, stifling under its blanket of carbon-monoxide. It appears to be without rationale, without centre, without unity, without any common objective and, need it be said, without beauty or order. Her Majesty's Stationery Office puts it thus, in their statistical survey for 1976 entitled *Social Trends* –

... seven conurbations account for a major part of the population of Great Britain. In 1974 their total resident populations combined amounted to 17·3 millions. This compares with a total for Great Britain of 54·4 millions, so that in all about one-third of the population of Great Britain lives in these areas which themselves comprise less than 3% of the total land area.

So over 17 million of our people live in less than 3% of the total land area of the United Kingdom, herded together in tower blocks, scarcely able to move in the streets or stand in the tube train, breathing foetid air. In Yorkshire the cows and the grouse do better – one cow to an acre of pasture land, two grouse to an acre of moor. Karl Marx, quoted by Professor Galbraith (op. cit.), says,

... the bourgeoisie has created enormous cities, has greatly increased the urban population as compared with the rural, and has thus rescued a considerable part of the population from the idiocy of rural life ... during its rule of scarce one hundred years, it has created more massive and more colossal productive forces than have all preceding generations together ...

There could be no more telling illustration of the extent to which Karl Marx was a child of his time. Many of us would be glad enough to be back to our 'rural idiocy'.

For over 17 million people in this country there is no chance of the return to 'rural idiocy' except as the unintended consequence of some nameless holocaust. What then are we to say of the giant conurbation swallowing up agricultural land, subjecting its inhabitants to concrete imprisonment, pouring out its deadly fumes into the atmosphere?

Perhaps the strangest thing about it is that it just happens. A piecemeal development here, a new road there, an industrial estate on some spare ground, a supermarket – and behold, the one-time inhabitants of a modest town with its clubs and pubs and shops find themselves part of a huge, amorphous conurbation. It is symptomatic of our age that having banished the demons from the woods and the streams and the hilltop cultic site, we perceive them now at work in the inner-most structures of our society, causing town councillors to make decisions the outcome of which they do not per-ceive, harnessing technological skills to developments we do not want, imposing upon millions of our people conditions of life which they have not desired.

Our warfare, as we have often seen in this book, is not against flesh and blood but against principalities and powers; against the rulers of the darkness of this world; against spiritual wickedness in high places. With-out seeming to disparage the well-intentioned efforts of those who attend to the problems thus created, the problems may well be by their nature insoluble.

Professor Galbraith delivered himself of what seemed to me an extraordinary judgement when, in the course of his television broadcasts, he suggested that the prob-lems of the inner cities could be solved by one thing – more money. We may indeed re-locate the problems by pouring the money in, but it would need someone either incurably optimistic or unaware of the real situation to suppose that more money alone can make our great con-urbations centres of culture and ease, of gracious living and creative community. The conurbation is a sign of our time, a sign of those mysterious processes at work in the world which can divert even the most well-intentioned enterprises to an altogether undesirable end. The city, a place of security, a market for the exchange of goods, an assembly of skills and crafts and arts, has become by some sinister progression an imprisoning, de-humanizing, altogether unlovely 'urban aggregate'.

Do we then just await the holocaust and a new Stone Age which lies the other side of it? Are we altogether trapped in an age-old circular movement which assigns great urban civilizations to the dust and launches new ones on their way? It is said that Jesus wept over the city. The city was Jerusalem, a city of modest size, impressive indeed to the Galilean disciples who had never seen such great buildings but unimpressive by the standards of Rome and Athens and Babylon. Jesus wept over it simply for the bigotry and the blindness which was exhibited there; wept over it because he saw in his mind's eye the day when it would be circled with armies, would be set alight and torn down leaving not one stone upon another because it had not recognized the day of its visitation.

It is a matter of continuing argument whether Mark 13 and its parallels in the other gospels predict or simply reflect the awful fate which overtook Jerusalem. But it certainly happened. The armies of Titus dragged their great siege trains up the road from Jericho. The zealots and their associates fought a good fight but the end was inevitable. The city ringed with armies went up in smoke; thousands upon thousands died of famine or violence; only a few escaped to continue the battle elsewhere. For those who lived through this disaster and for those who viewed it from afar, the fall of Jerusalem was more than a disaster, it was a sign. It was a sign, some of them thought, of God's ultimate intervention in human affairs, of the end of the world and the return of the Son of Man. They were mistaken in terms of a strict timetable and parts of the New Testament reflect the tension and uncertainty which gripped the early Christian communities as they struggled with the recognition that it was not to be so. 'Where is the promise of his coming?' they said. 'For since the fathers fell asleep, all things continue as they were from the beginning of creation.'

They were wrong in so far as those early believers foreshortened the timetable. It could hardly have been otherwise – our Lord himself did not claim exact knowledge of the time of the end. It was hidden in the secret councils of God. But in terms of the profound theology of the Bible, they were not wrong. Those who penetrated most deeply into the nature of the human condition, knew that there were problems to which there were no solutions. It is one of the assumptions of a technological age that all problems are there to be solved; it is only a question of a new mechanical device or a better educational system or, as Professor Galbraith would seem to suggest, more money. The conurbation in that sense is indeed a sign of the times and let him who runs read. It is the sign of a defeated civilization which awaits its end as indeed Jerusalem awaited its end in the first century of our era. But for the Christian that is not in itself a sign of despair. His confidence is in God, not in man. The only perfect solution to any problem was not one which would have occurred to our unassisted intellect – the birth of a baby in Bethlehem. Neither are we likely to be able to comprehend the nature of the final solution. Jesus wept over the city and for the lives within it that would be engulfed by sword and fire, but through the smoke and the fire he discerned another city,

> the holy city, new Jerusalem, coming down from God out of heaven, prepared as a bride adorned for her husband. And I heard a great voice out of heaven saying, Behold, the tabernacle of God is with men, and he will dwell with them, and they shall be his people, and God himself shall be with them, and be their God. And God shall wipe away all tears from their eyes; and there shall be no more death, neither sorrow, nor crying, neither shall there be any more pain: for the former things are passed away.
> (Revelation 21:2–4, Authorized Version.)

Alas for our conurbations. Alleluia for our God.

THE BURNING BUSH

I resist the tendency to regard the twentieth century as something utterly distinct from preceding centuries in the history of mankind. All too easily we arrogate to ourselves a certain privileged position from which to view the human condition and to draw conclusions from it. But the tower block is not an entirely new phenomenon, nor the freedom fighter, nor the young vandal or Big Brother. The signs of our own times have been often enough the signs of other times as well. I recoil instinctively, therefore, from the title of the three-volumed Oxford paperback, *The Twentieth Century Mind*. It is an admirable book but the title flatters us. There is, however, one point at which it might be said that the twentieth century is distinctive. The authors C. B. Cox and A. E. Dyson allude to the discoveries of Freud, Darwin, Frazer and William James, and then go on to say:

> All these developments, highly complicated and needing detailed treatment to be understood precisely, are part of a huge shift in the climate of opinion. The departure of God from ordinary social thinking is the starting-point for many twentieth-century writers. It was increasingly to be assumed, along with Comte, that theology and metaphysics belonged to earlier phases of human thought, and that the new 'positive' age – the age of pragmatism and sociology – would study all moral and social questions without reference to, and without assumptions concerning, religious belief. 'God is dead' meant, of course, not that God really was dead and required an obituary, but that the idea of God was dead as a social power. Where, however, was

man, without his creator? Was he more, or less, free on his own? If man knows only his own consciousness and lives without God, then what in fact does he know? The 'self' may prove isolated, locked in a prison, hearing, in T. S. Eliot's words, 'the key turn in the door once and turn once only.' In Conrad and James nothing exists except as it is seen by someone viewing the world from his own perspective. In Conrad the nihilism implicit in such attitudes is brought to the surface and shown for what it is. For him civilization is an illusion, an arbitrary set of rules and judgements, a house of cards built over an abyss. 'A man that is born', says Stein in Lord Jim, 'falls into a dream like a man who falls into the sea.'

(Cox and Dyson, *The Twentieth Century Mind*, Oxford.)

Mark Twain is reputed to have said when having his attention drawn to a premature obituary notice, 'The report is grossly exaggerated.' The same might be said of God's obituary – the report is grossly exaggerated. But it will also have to be said that it is widely believed, and it is the belief as distinct perhaps from the fact that colours our thinking and makes us feel that our civilization is 'a house of cards built over an abyss'.

Faith in a living God indeed persists in the hearts of thousands of millions of twentieth-century men and persists often with a newly acquired intensity, but our authors could be right in saying the idea of God is dead as a social power. His existence is a matter for private conjecture; the church is a sect; faith is an option. The secular society does not necessarily prohibit religion and its attempts to do so have signally failed even in otherwise all-powerful totalitarian systems. But faith in the living God is no longer part of the fabric of society. It is not one of the assumptions upon which national and social affairs are conducted. The parliamentary private secretary may be a man of faith, he may open the windows of his heart towards Jerusalem every day, but once he is in his office other considerations take over, and he is involved in a whole complex of nice adjustments in which, so he assumes, God is not interested.

There is, of course, nothing new about private conviction being at variance with public policy. What is new, so our authors suggest, is that it is quite inevitable – the only things that can persuade the secular man are secular arguments. Atheism becomes the formal stance of the believer and the unbeliever alike. Comte was right – theology and metaphysics seem to belong to earlier phases of human thought. It is in this loss of dimension that we may perceive the origins of so much of the pain and confusion of twentieth-century civilization – so richly provided outwardly, so famished inwardly.

So, we may ask, is there any burning bush in our wilderness which may revive within us faith in the God of Abraham, Isaac and Jacob? I put the question this way because it is with this issue that the narrative of the burning bush in the book of Exodus is apparently concerned:

Moses was minding the flock of his father-in-law Jethro, priest of Midian. He led the flock along the side of the wilderness and came to Horeb, the mountain of God. There the angel of the LORD appeared to him in the flame of a burning bush. Moses noticed that, although the bush was on fire, it was not being burnt up; so he said to himself, 'I must go across to see this wonderful sight. Why does not the bush burn away?' When the LORD saw that Moses had turned aside to look, he called to him out of the bush, 'Moses, Moses.' And Moses answered, 'Yes, I am here.' God said, 'Come no nearer; take off your sandals; the

place where you are standing is holy ground.' Then he said,
'I am the God of your forefathers, the God of Abraham, the
God of Isaac, the God of Jacob.' Moses covered his face,
for he was afraid to gaze on God.
(Exodus 3:1–6, New English Bible.)

The treatment of this remarkable passage in the com-
mentaries ranges from learned discussions about the
vegetation one might expect to find in the wilderness
to an examination of the Hebrew word for bush (*seneh*)
and its possible punning association with the name of the
mountain where the theophany was believed to have
taken place. The commentators are content to say either
that it was an actual occurrence or that it was simply a
means of giving expression to Moses' internal colloquies
with God; they leave the profounder considerations to
the theologians, the mystics and the poets.

Thus, for example, Elizabeth Barrett Browning in a
familiar passage from *Aurora Leigh*, speaks of that inner
appropriation of the natural world which is available to
us all:

Earth's crammed with heaven,
And every common bush afire with God;
But only he who sees, takes off his shoes –
The rest sit round it and pluck blackberries.

Robert Browning put it a slightly different way:

How can we guard our unbelief,
Make it bear fruit to us – the problem here.
Just when we are safest, there's a sunset-touch,
A fancy from a flower-bell, someone's death,
A chorus-ending from Euripides, –
And that's enough for fifty hopes and fears
As old and new at once as nature's self,
To rap and knock and enter in our soul,

Take hands and dance there, a fantastic ring,
Round the ancient idol, on his base again, –
The grand Perhaps!

Both passages illustrate a theme familiar in the pages of holy scripture and outside it. The prophet might see an almond tree or a basket of rotten fruit or a pot boiling and receive messages thereby for transmission to the people of his day. Brother Lawrence speaks of that transforming experience which he received:

> when seeing a tree stripped of its leaves, and considering that within a little time the leaves would be renewed, and after that the flowers and fruit appear, he received a high view of the Providence and power of God, which has never since been effaced from his soul. That this view had set him perfectly loose from the world, and kindled in him such a love for God, that he could not tell whether it had increased in above forty years that he had lived since.

These are perfectly legitimate interpretations of the Exodus narrative. Most of us have had our moments when we felt that earth was crammed with heaven. But I doubt if they do justice to the centrality given to this event by the sacred writers themselves and the far reaching consequences of it in the subsequent history of mankind.

There is a curious blank in the Pentateuch between Joseph's death and the birth of Moses, corresponding to a period of as long as between two hundred and four hundred years. There was presumably nothing to record. But the form in which the early history of Israel is preserved in the sacred writings invites us to ask the question, what of the faith which Abraham, Isaac and Jacob had bequeathed to their successors? To what extent was the faith of Moses, so dramatically revived by the sight of the burning bush, continuous with or even consonant with the faith of his forefathers as described in the book of Genesis? To this question the book of Exodus gives a strong, although to the modern scholar unenlightening answer – it was the God of Abraham, the God of Isaac and the God of Jacob who spoke to Moses from the burning bush, a God presumably long-submerged beneath the secularities of Israel's existence in Egypt and the secularities of Moses' existence as the adopted son of Pharaoh's daughter and a member of Pharaoh's court.

For two or three hundred years, so it would seem, the Israelites had herded their cattle and laboured on Pharaoh's artefacts, and Moses had been involved in the affairs of government, entirely without any means of exhibiting or living by their faith in the God of Abraham, Isaac and Jacob.

The incident of the burning bush is an incident entirely mysterious, which does not yield at all to historical investigation and only with difficulty to theological reflection. Something new and unpredictable but highly significant happened, and we who live out our lives three thousand years and more after that event are different people because of it. The burning bush was a life-changing, world-changing sign penetrating the secularity of a people in bondage and breaking open the mind of a man long since trapped in the routines of everyday existence and, worse still, contented with them.

Learned comment on the nature of vegetation in the wilderness, and even comparisons with the experience of prophets and mystics, have to yield to the central mystery by which God makes himself known to a man and changes the course of human history from within a burning bush. Perhaps amongst the modern poets Norman Nicholson puts it as well as anybody in his poem *The Burning Bush* (Religious Education Press):

> When Moses, musing in the desert, found
> The thorn bush spiking up from the hot ground,
> And saw the branches, on a sudden, bear
> The crackling yellow barberries of fire,
>
> He searched his learning and imagination
> For any logical, neat explanation,
> And turned to go, but turned again and stayed,
> And faced the fire and knew it for his God.
>
> I too have seen the briar alight like a coal,
> The love that burns, the flesh that's ever whole,
> And many times have turned and left it there,
> Saying: 'It's prophecy – but metaphor'.
>
> But stinging tongues like John the Baptist shout:
> 'That this is metaphor is no way out.
> It's dogma too, or you make God a liar;
> The bush is still a bush, and fire is fire.'

This is no metaphor. The bush is still a bush and fire is fire, and the experience remains an ingredient of human existence with which every son of man has to reckon – for his blessing or his bane.

That is all very well, you may say, for the second millennium BC. But what about us in our wilderness in the second millennium AD? Indeed there are those who experience earth crammed with heaven; there are indeed those who perceive within the natural the supernatural; there are those who live out their temporal lives on the basis of the eternal. But where is the universal sign which can assemble this variegated experience into a significant whole?

No man ought to be content with a private vision. If it is real, as the prophets saw, it must be communicable, it must be for all, it must be for the saving of the world, not just a Moses here or an Isaiah there, a Jeremiah in Jerusalem or an Ezekiel in Babylon. Signs of the times there are in abundance, but where is the Sign of our time?

I write at Eastertide with the Passiontide laments and the Easter alleluias sounding in my ears. A substantial proportion of television time is being given to a six-hour film on the life of Jesus of Nazareth. In front of me I have the leading article from a mass circulation newspaper entitled 'Good Friday's Message'. In thousands of churches the bells will be ringing and in many a city hall 'secular' choirs will be singing the Matthew Passion, or the Seven Words from the Cross, or Stainer's *Crucifixion*. Through a million stained-glass windows the sun will shine illuminating a figure which will be different in each case but will without difficulty be identified by all. Here indeed is a bush burning in the wilderness which is not consumed.

A leading official of the USSR was brave enough to say, 'We shall have to live with this religion for another thousand years.' Certain facts concerning the life of Christ are not in dispute. Whatever the uncertainties of detail, it is almost universally conceded that a man named Jesus of Nazareth handed on certain teachings to his disciples, acquired (rather unwillingly) the reputation of being a wonder-worker, lived for most of his life in Galilee, encountered bitter opposition from the religious hierarchy in Jerusalem, was accused of blasphemy and sentenced to death by the Procurator, Pontius Pilate. He was buried in a tomb belonging to Joseph of Arimathæa, but on the following Sunday morning the tomb was empty – and has remained empty ever since. Through a variety of experiences his disciples became convinced that he had risen from the dead, and their successors have been proclaiming it ever since – in word and deed, in drama and liturgy, in art and music.

It seems that he cannot be hid, that he burns still in many a wilderness, personal and corporate, and men still hear through him the voice of the God of Abraham, Isaac and Jacob. So amidst the many signs of the times with their fragmentary and fugitive messages we ask whether this may not be the universal Sign. It is a sign to us of a total human failure, depicted in the blindness and the bigotry of official organs of government and in the horrifying venality of the church of the day, and at the same time a sign of God's victory over the adverse forces of the world, embracing the whole of history in a single redemptive act and assuring us of that consummation when the kingdoms of this world shall become the kingdom of God, and of his Christ.

Perhaps we ought not to be surprised at this conclusion when we remember the prophecy of Simeon, 'This child is destined to be a sign.' We look for portents in the sky, but in an obscure corner of our wilderness there is a bush which still burns with fire and, so we believe, the creator of all the earth speaks from it. In the unexampled life of Jesus of Nazareth God's word to mankind became flesh, and those who will can behold him, full of grace and truth. When that happens to a man, no wilderness can seem quite the same again. This world itself becomes the house of God and the gateway to heaven.

CONCLUSION

Certain conclusions have been borne in upon my mind as I have struggled with the signs of our time, and they are as follows:

1. The so-called 'social questions' of our age are wrongly named. On the whole they are not particularly of our age at all, they are not predominantly social either. When everything has been said about the distinctiveness of the social structures of a particular epoch they in fact do little more than reflect the perennial tensions within the human psyche itself. It is of the essence of wisdom to know that there is nothing new under the sun. 'Lord save me from the hasty conclusion that I am wiser than my fathers.' What is peculiar about the twentieth century is that it tends to identify these tensions in predominantly social terms and thus in a way evades the central challenge to ourselves. It is not the welfare state alone which has produced an unhealthy dependence upon others; it is the steadily growing conviction due, one must presume, to the sociological thinking of the last two centuries, that the individual is powerless to change the course of events. Economic determinism, amongst all the other determinisms, has bitten deeply into our view of things and produces a certain kind of apathy which just waits nervelessly for some secular god to redeem us.

2. It has become evident to me that the secular god cannot redeem us. The social questions are beyond us. There is a sense in which we are less well-equipped than

our forefathers to penetrate to the springs of human action and to motivate some change there. We have lost a lot of wisdom in acquiring knowledge.

These questions were beyond the wise men of the past as well, but part of their wisdom consisted in the acknowledgement that this was so. They felt the profundity of those questions which trouble the human soul. They were not foolish enough to imagine that the solution to the problem lay within their grasp. This is presumably why the ancient world tended to look outwards or upwards for succour. Like the children on William Golding's island they were aware of the destructive forces that ravaged this world and looked out across the beach for a deliverer. They were not necessarily religious men; they simply left a little room for mystery and in their attitude to life often reflected a certain 'faith'.

3. For whatever reason, there has been during the last decade a new public awareness of the demonic in human affairs. It has sometimes taken bizarre forms and has in many cases been blatantly recidivist; covens of witches appear on sacred hilltops, black masses are celebrated, spirits are raised out of the abyss and the unhappy victims of this activity find themselves in a law court or a mental home. Before we dismiss it altogether we ought perhaps to weigh the possibility that this is a kind of rebuke to the crude materialism which surrounds us, a reminder that our warfare is not always against flesh and blood, but against principalities and powers, spiritual wickedness in high places. There is indeed something demonic about the way in which we do things we do not intend, we achieve results we do not desire and move headlong into the abyss which we see perfectly clearly before us. We

have need of light if we are to confront darkness. We have need of God if we are to resist the devil. We have need of grace if we are to face up to the dangerous compulsions of our own nature. In short, as our Lord knew full well, we are not always in control of our actions. There are some who are ill and some who are 'possessed'. Before Christ won his victories over men he had to win his victory over the devil.

4. The church must seem to many readers of this book an irrelevance in public affairs, however powerful still in individual hearts and lives. But the church has never been content with a private role, nor indeed can it be, given our Lord's unceasing emphasis upon 'the kingdom'. Nothing less than the subjection of all human affairs to the sovereignty of God is the aim of his mission and the mission of his church. Before that prospect the mind is apt to collapse, when we look at our little introverted congregations, our tame compromises, our feeble grasp of the eternal, our fluctuating faith and our fearfulness before the seemingly invincible political, economic and industrial structures of the world.

Yet even to the most disparaging gaze the church exists. It has a continuous history from the time of Abraham to our own day long outliving powerful empires with which it has been surrounded, still worshipping the God of Abraham, Isaac and Jacob. We look not to the things which are seen – the tottering structures of the institutional church – but to the things which are unseen – the unchanging will of God, the consistent theology of the Bible and that inner spirit which against all the odds always sustains and sometimes revives the witness of the people of God.

The musical *Fiddler on the Roof* ends with a scene of a

little group of dishevelled Jews taking their few miserable possessions with them, moving out from the little town they had loved to a new world against a chiaroscuro of skyscrapers and power stations, of aeroplanes and space rockets, of factories and war machines. It was an infinitely poignant commentary on the sad but strangely triumphant journey of the people of God leaving one civilization behind and moving to another, always on the move, but not knowing whither.

It could be that the church is more important than the worldling or even the churchman may be prepared to concede in the ultimate triumph of God over all the earth.

> We through the generations came
> Here by a way we do not know
> From the fields of Abraham,
> And still the road is scarce begun.
> To hazard and to danger go
> The sallying generations all
> Where the imperial highways run.
> And our songs and legends call
> The hazard and the danger good.

(Edwin Muir, *Collected Poems*, Faber & Faber.)